NORTH YORK
MOORS AND COAST

Richard Musgrave

• *25 circular walks including country inns* •

DALESMAN

Dalesman Publishing Company

Stable Courtyard, Broughton Hall,

Skipton, North Yorkshire BD23 3AE

First Edition 1997
Reprinted 2001

Text © Richard Musgrave

Illustrations © Geoff Cowton

Maps by Jeremy Ashcroft

Cover: Robin Hood's Bay

A British Library Cataloguing in Publication record
is available for this book

ISBN 1 85568 087 4

Other books in this series:
Pub Walks in the Yorkshire Dales
by Richard Musgrave (ISBN 1 85568 103 X)
Pub Walks in the Lake District
by Terry Marsh (ISBN 185568 111 0)

Printed by Amadeus Press, Cleckheaton,

Walks

PUBLISHER'S NOTE

The information given in this book has been provided in good faith and is intended only as a general guide. Whilst all reasonable efforts have been made to ensure that details were correct at the time of publication, the author and Dalesman Publishing Company Ltd cannot accept any responsibility for inaccuracies. It is the responsibility of individuals undertaking outdoor activities to approach the activity with caution and, especially if inexperienced, to do so under appropriate supervision. They should also carry the appropriate equipment and maps, be properly clothed and have adequate footwear. The sport described in this book is strenuous and individuals should ensure that they are suitably fit before embarking upon it.

Some of the pubs mentioned in the book open only between Easter and October so telephone numbers have been included to assist forward planning. Permission to park cars at any of the pubs must be obtained in advance.

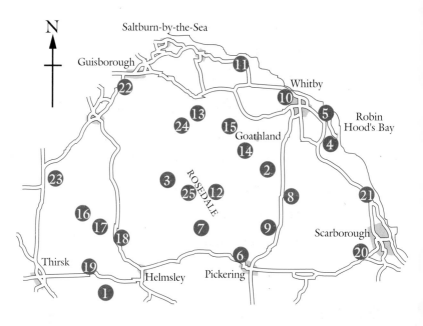

This book is respectfully dedicated to my wonderful
friends Trevor, John and Lynda.

Thanks to Peter N Walker of Ampleforth and Cheryl
Pawley of Horsforth.

FOREWORD

A three-handed foreword may seem a little unusual, but the three of us have acted as a "backing group" for Richard Musgrave in this publication. There has been some degree of involvement in almost all the walks included. Naturally we were delighted when he asked us to jointly write the foreword.

The North York Moors National Park encompasses a variety of scenery ranging from the stark high moor tops to the fertile valleys, from the dramatic western escarpment running northwards from Sutton Bank to the equally dramatic seascape around Robin Hood's Bay. The walks in this book will give you a taste of all these experiences – plus the pleasure of a meal or drink in welcoming hostelries.

Of our own experiences we vividly recall the week spent in Rosedale in February 1996, researching many of these walks when virtually the whole of the country was paralysed by snow. Miraculously the North York Moors escaped and the coast was bathed in brilliant sunshine. It proved to be a good omen for the book.

The book is more than just a stride-by-stride description of walks from A to B and back. Richard's lively and inquiring mind ensures there's a feast of historical and geographical information for the reader to absorb and which can add so much more interest to a walk.

Richard's book brings back pleasant memories for each of us. We are sure it will provide them for you as well.

Trevor Kitson, John and Lynda Pickering

INTRODUCTION

The North York Moors National Park covers 553 square miles (1432 sq. kilometres) encompassing large tracts of heather moorland, green valleys and miles of glorious, undulating coastline. The highest point is a modest 1500 ft (457m). It has become an area largely dependent on tourism – although farming continues to be the major industry. Potash is still mined at the Boulby Mine, between Loftus and Staithes, but years ago the area was synonymous with other industries, as men toiled to extract other minerals such as whinstone, jet, alum and ironstone. Fishing remains an important occupation in some of the coastal villages.

Of these, the production of aluminium sulphate which preceded the large scale ironstone activities was the principal operation, employing hundreds of men over several centuries. The site of the Peak Alum Works at Ravenscar, preserved by the National Trust, is a must for those interested in industrial history. It is a fascinating place and worthy of the long descent and ascent.

Seek out the many locations described in the following pages – there's a wealth of information awaiting the curious mind. Above all, enjoy the walks and the refreshments which will undoubtedly follow.

Happy walking.

Richard Musgrave

GEOFF COWTON

A childhood spent in inner-city Bradford did little to prepare Geoffrey Cowton for the captivating beauty of the countryside. So the effect of a school geography trip involving a walk from Grassington to Malham was dramatic. He says: "The trip was literally an eye-opener for me, having come from a place where there were no fields and we had only a tiny garden. I loved all of it."

The result was a life-long love affair with beautiful scenery and now he spends as much time as possible roaming the Dales and the Lake District, gathering material for his distinctive paintings and drawings.

The finished works are produced at his Glendale Studio in King Cross, Halifax, working from on-the-spot sketches and meticulous notes backed up by location photographs.

Geoff Cowton has drawn all the pubs featured in this book and also those in the other Dalesman books of this series: Pub Walks in the Yorkshire Dales and Pub Walks in the Lake District.

THE BLACK SWAN

OLDSTEAD

An outing promising much interest and enjoyment. The walk takes in the charming villages of Oldstead and Wass and visits Byland Abbey and the Mount Snever Observatory.

DISTANCE:
5$\frac{1}{2}$ miles
ALLOW:
2$\frac{1}{2}$-3 hours
MAP: OS
Outdoor Leisure
Map 26 Western
area, SW Sheet
PARKING: At
the Black Swan
by prior
arrangement.
Tel 01347
868387.

Cistercian monks established the abbey at Byland in 1177. They transformed the surrounding lands, clearing, draining and cultivating the rough ground and developing a flourishing wool trade with flocks of nearly 10,000 sheep. The abbey was a centre of importance and activity in the area until the Dissolution of the Monasteries in 1538, when there were 25 monks and the abbot in residence.

The site was granted to Sir William Pickering in 1540 and was eventually transferred to the Wombwells of nearby Newburgh Priory. In 1924 the ruins became the responsibility of the Ministry of Works. The abbey has a particularly splendid west front with a great rose window measuring 26ft (8m) across.

Oldstead has had two other names in the past. The Cistercian monks of Byland who lived there from 1144 to 1177 named it 'Stocking', which meant a clearing in the woods used for pasture. When they moved to Byland the settlement was known as *Veterum Locum* – the old place, surely the origin of the name.

O L D S T E A D

The village has a population of around 50, and rests below two extended ridges of the Hambleton Hills. On one of these ridges stands a tower built by John Wormald of Oldstead Hall to commemorate Queen Victoria's Coronation. This is the Mount Snever Observatory, where on a clear day views extend across northern England from Staxton Wold near Filey in the east to the fells of Cumbria in the west.

The other hill situated a mile north of the village is called Scotch Corner, a name synonymous with a battle in 1322 between the armies of Edward II and invading Scots. Edward was defeated and fled to York, leaving the Scots to ransack the abbey at Byland.

Oldstead has a former Methodist chapel, now a house, and a very good pub – the Black Swan, where the motto is 'Don't drink the beck dry, call at the old Oldstead inn instead'!

The walk commences from the Black Swan at Oldstead (GR531 799), heading towards the magnificent ruin at Byland. The Cistercian foundation, close to the village, is the initial landmark. The ruins are extensive, indicating a huge development for its time. Note especially the enormous rose window at the abbey's west end. At the junction veer left to follow the road in the direction of the neighbouring village of Wass, which is entered after a pronounced left hand bend. A building on the right displays a datestone of 1897.

Arriving at the cross-roads (GR555 794) alongside the Wombwell Arms, swing left to enter a lane, signposted as a dead-end. Prior to making this maneouvre, note the building beyond the cross-roads which displays a fine clock and bell turret. This was formerly the village school and now functions as St. Thomas' church.

Continue up the lane for about five minutes. As it levels out and housing development ends, the lane enters Abbey Bank Wood, continuing as a clear broad track. Pass a small pond on the right, heading uphill towards a gate on a pronounced bend (GR550 795). At the gate a signpost indicates Cam Farm and Observatory, the latter being the eventual destination and approximate half way point of the outing.

Beyond the gate follow the wire fence on the left until this merges with a dilapidated stone wall. Follow the wall uphill for a short distance to a stile.

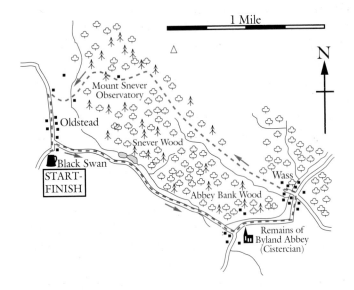

Cross this then follow the broad, right hand track between an avenue of rhododendrons. A short distance afterwards ignore an obvious and tempting left fork situated at the bottom of an incline. You must continue upwards! At the top the track levels out and threads its way through a conifer plantation.

Pass a waymarked gate on the right (GR541 805), proceeding alongside the wall with the trees to your left. Follow the wall until it is replaced by a fence. At this point veer left towards the observatory (GR538 805), using one of the several narrow paths threading through the coppice – all leading to the intended location. Allow about five minutes for this detour.

An inscription on the tower reads: "John Wormald, in the

first year of the reign of Queen Victoria, caused the observatory to be erected." A badly-eroded sonnet on the front of the tower is worthy of further attention (and possible restoration?).

The ramble re-commences with a steep descent from the front left hand (south) corner of the tower. A well defined path wriggles through mixed woodland, eventually merging with a broad forestry track. Turn right and follow this track for a short way to arrive at a T-junction (GR534 806). Swing left, ignoring the signpost pointing in the opposite direction.

Pass through a gateway, then follow the access road straight ahead, to a junction – turn left, then left again at the next junction to re-enter the tidy village of Oldstead by following the road straight on beyond a slight incline.

As you pass Scawling Farm, look behind and beyond the house opposite – Mount Snever Observatory should be on view. The village's former Methodist chapel has been converted to a house and look out for the Victorian post box set into a cottage on the right.

THE MALLYAN SPOUT

GOATHLAND

Roaring rivers, winding railways and a 75ft waterfall plus the much-visited villages of Goathland and Grosmont to see and enjoy en route.

DISTANCE: 7 miles
ALLOW: 3½-4½ hours
MAP: OS Outdoor Leisure Map 27 Eastern area, NE Sheet.
PARKING: Car park, Goathland.

NOTE: Careful navigation will be needed on sections of this outing.

Situated between two vibrant watercourses, West Beck and Eller Beck, the once remote village of Goathland has become a major tourist attraction. The reason for its popularity is the TV series Heartbeat, Goathland being the fictitious Aidensfield.

The village is spacious and incorporates large areas of grassed verges which are kept in order by the village gardeners – moorland sheep.

There are several hotels, including the Mallyan Spout (TEL 01947 896206), which is named after the 75ft waterfall situated to the rear of the premises.

Commence the walk from the large free car-park in Goathland, turning left along the road and passing the public toilets. After 50m at a signpost (Grosmont) turn left through a gate and head off along a pleasant grassed path.

Reaching a point where a road runs between adjacent gates, swing right following the road to a junction

(GR831 017). At the junction turn left – signposted
Beck Hole and follow the road a short distance to a
public footpath (signpost) on the right. Follow this into
a narrow, enclosed lane, then after crossing a stile you get
the first view of the North York Moors railway. Hop over
a second stile and descend the steps to pass under the
railway, then cross over the footbridge.

*The river is the Murk Esk, its belligerent waters forcing
their way through a narrow channel in the bedrock. The
scene resembles the Strid in Wharfedale. The river is
powerful and menacing at this spot. A tombstone marks the
tragic death of 16-year-old Sydney Porritt, who drowned
here in June 1908.*

As well as being dangerous, the river is also quite

spectacular, with several tumbling waterfalls as the river curves wildly between two railway bridges.

Parting company with the river the path rises to a seat, before continuing alongside the wall to your left. After a short distance (close to a large ivy-clad tree) swing away right instead of making towards the farmhouse (Hill Farm) ahead. Make for a wall angle 200m to the right of the farmhouse, cutting off a corner (GR824 024).

From the wall angle follow the wall to your left to emerge on a road where you turn right. Head towards Hollin Garth Farm on the left and pass through an unmarked metal gate, just beyond the farm buildings. One is immediately convinced that ramblers aren't welcome. A lack of waymarks, often a surplus of mud and a sign which boasts "our dogs bite", confirm suspicions.

Proceed to a second gate (stile on left) then following the same line, pass through the right of two gates, walking with a hedge on your left. Pass through a farmyard to a farm access road where you swing left. After 300m close to Green End Farm (GR825 035) veer right at a public bridleway sign.

Pass through a rickety gate, then enter a narrow lane slightly to the left. Emerging from this short enclosed section, follow the signpost to Grosmont, descending to a footbridge before continuing along a well-defined track. Two waymarked stiles are negotiated in quick succession, followed by several others, then a footbridge is crossed, before entering deciduous Crag Cliff Wood (GR826 042). The path is clear – you can't go wrong.

Notice the packhorse trail as you pass through the woods. Emerging from the woods continue to follow the causey slabs, until merging with a metalled track which is followed downhill to a green painted gate. Grosmont railway sidings will have been evident for some minutes.

Pass through the gate (GR829 047) and immediately before reaching a 'Ford' sign, swing right and cross a footbridge. The path rises through woodland, emerging onto a road opposite Park Villa (1877). Turn left, downhill into the unique railway village of Grosmont. This is the half-way point and the Station Tavern makes an ideal refreshment stop. During the high season the village is understandably busy. Be patient!

The return leg commences by walking between the viewing area and the cottages situated adjacent to the signal box. Cross the footbridge, then veer left – signposted Goathland. The tunnel directly ahead was originally used by horses pulling trains in the pre-steam days.

Pass St Matthew's church, go up the incline and follow signposts for the Grosmont Rail Trail. Shortly after passing the "header" water tank, make for the seat. Superb retrospective views of Grosmont are presented and shouldn't be missed. From the seat turn through the gate, passing the engine sidings which boast an assortment of railway memorabilia and spare parts.

The return to Goathland follows the route of Stephenson's original horse-drawn railway, and needs little detailed explanation.

Along the way you'll pass the brick-built former Esk Valley Methodist Chapel (GR823 044) opposite a row of cottages, built originally to house men employed in the ironstone industry. Approaching the cottages, you'll see away to the left, Hudson's Deviation Line, which enabled steam-hauled locomotives to be used.

Continue along the railway until some steps are encountered. At this juncture swing right across the new footbridge, then straight on, following the waymarkers to Goathland.

A plaque marks the site of the long-disappeared Beck Hole Station (GR820 022). It reads: "This is the site of Beck Hole Station which was closed in 1865 following the building of a new railway between Goathland and

Grosmont. However, since the rails were left in place, it was temporarily reopened 1908-14 to serve an autocar service during the summer from Whitby to Beck Hole."

If preferred a short detour to visit the quaint, hidden-away village of Beck Hole can be made. If you elect to visit Beck Hole resume your journey to Goathland by turning right just beyond the Birch Hall Inn and enter a signposted track which returns you to the railway. Turn left (signposted Goathland).

On approaching a cottage dated 1789 on the left, turn right, making for a gate, signposted "To the Mallyan". Head across the field towards a pleasant beck-side path. Cross a stile and begin a stiff climb, following the stone staircase. Reaching the top of the staircase, pause awhile (to get your breath back) and enjoy the wonderful retrospective views.

Proceed, following the fence on the right. Eventually the path descends to a signpost to Goathland. This is the eventual route but first continue straight on to visit the spectacular 75ft waterfall – Mallyan Spout (GR825 009). The area around the waterfall is heavily cloaked with bluebells in season.

After visiting the waterfall, retrace footsteps back to the Goathland signpost and commence the second climb of the day. The Mallyan Spout Hotel is at the top. Turn left through the sprawling village to the car park.

Goathland's fastidiously maintained Victorian railway station is worth seeking out. This can be reached by continuing along the road beyond the carpark for about five minutes.

FEVERSHAM ARMS

__N__o book of walks could omit an outing set in beautiful Farndale, but be warned, in season traffic can be chaotic as everyone heads there to see the wonderful daffodils.

DISTANCE:
3³/₄ miles
ALLOW: 2¹/₂
hours –
including church
visit.
MAP: OS
Outdoor Leisure
Map 26 North
York Moors
Western Area
SW sheet
PARKING: At
pub by prior
arrangement
(Tel 01751
433206) or
roadside.

Farndale is a peaceful, scenic valley in the centre of the North York Moors National Park. The valley houses a scattered farming community and has two centres of habitation – Low Mills, where there were formerly two corn mills, and Church Houses, located as the name implies, close to the church. Farndale is famous for its displays of wild daffodils thought to have been planted by monks from outlying granges of Rievaulx Abbey.

In the summer the area attracts thousands of visitors. To avoid the crowds this walk will be best undertaken outside the main season, or if you're intent on seeing the daffodils, start early in the day. The valley has twice been threatened by flooding but thankfully this was vigorously resisted. In 1914 there were plans for a reservoir to satisfy Hull's increasing demand for water, then in the 1960s a second scheme to flood the valley was mooted.

Start from the Feversham Arms, which offers bar meals, snacks and an a la carte menu in the restaurant, and turn left to follow the signpost Farndale – West side. This leads into a lane displaying a dead end road sign. After a short distance the metalled surface gives way to a rough track signposted Low Mill (ignore the sign to Cow Bank). Along the way is High Mill (GR668 971) – where there is a culinary oasis in the form of Poppy's Pantry (closed Wednesday) – and beyond this is a pleasant grass track alongside the infant River Dove. Don't cross the wooden footbridge unless a detour to the toilets or Post Office of Low Mill is necessary.

After the footbridge pass through the second gate and across the field towards a telegraph pole close to an oak tree. Follow the paved trod and go over a stile, partially hidden to the left side of a holly bush. After a second stile make directly towards the farm buildings ahead (GR675 956).

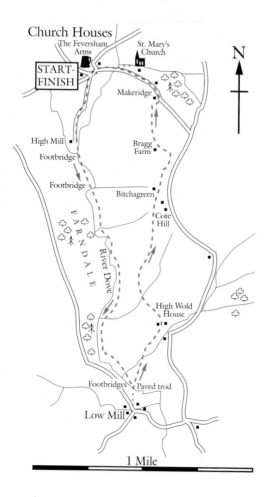

Church Houses

The Feversham Arms

St. Mary's Church

START-FINISH

N

Makeridge

High Mill

Footbridge

Bragg Farm

Footbridge

Bitchagreen

FARNDALE

River Dove

Cote Hill

High Wold House

Footbridges   Paved trod

Low Mill

1 Mile

Pass through the farmyard gate, swinging left as indicated to follow a direct line which eventually arrives at a double set of gates. Use the right-hand gate then walk along the field with the boundary to your left. After 50m pass through another gate, veer right and along the field edge with the boundary to your right. The high, flat-topped hill away to the left is Horn Ridge (330m).

Just short of the buildings is a wide gate. From here head diagonally left, across the field to a ladder stile and continue in front of the houses to another waymark; beyond is a second waymarked gate (GR675 965).

Pass straight through the confines of Bitchagreen Farm, over a stone step-stile and across the field. On reaching a farm track veer left, then proceed straight through Bragg Farm, following a signpost to Makeridge.

Walking directly ahead select the right-hand gate when two are encountered. Next make for a ladder stile in the left corner of the field. At this point turn 90 degrees right to a road where you turn left. (GR675 973).

The final half mile to Church Houses is on the road. Along the way the old village hall and the church of St. Mary are encountered, and a visit to the latter is recommended. The Feversham family of Duncombe Park, Helmsley, are featured at both locations.

THE BAY HOTEL

ROBIN HOOD'S BAY

Just three miles long yet full of interest. Long sections of shoreline and redundant railways ensure enjoyment throughout. Remember to watch the tides.

DISTANCE: 3 miles
ALLOW: 2 hours
MAP: O.S. Outdoor Leisure Map 27 Eastern area, NE Sheet
PARKING: Public car parks opposite Bay Hotel (Tel 01947 880278) and on site of a former railway station.

Robin Hood's Bay lies within the parish of Fylingdales. It is mentioned in the Domesday Book and has been designated a conservation area. This tiny coastal spot is quite important for long distance rambling, being sited on the Cleveland Way, and is the beginning – or end – of the Coast to Coast walk (from St. Bees, Cumbria), and is near the end of the Lyke Wake Walk, a 40-mile moorland tramp from Osmotherley.

Cottages in the village have been constructed from locally quarried stone. Formerly there were 12 inns; only three remain. Many cottages are holiday lets and consequently often empty in the winter. The village school closed in the 1960s and is now a Marine Activity Centre.

The railway, once one of the most scenically beautiful lines, travelled between Scarborough and Whitby. The line was one of the many which fell to Beeching's axe in the 1960s. A new village hall was built on the site. This incorporates the old station goods warehouse, while the waiting rooms and ticket office became a senior citizens' club. The signal box

is the coal merchant's office and the station master's house, a private residence. The remainder has formed a car park, catering for the considerable influx of summer visitors.

The original parish church (late 11th century) – known as the Old Church – occupies a prominent site overlooking the village. The church contains the original three-decker pulpit and box pews. Maidens' Garlands, reputedly carried at maidens' funerals and last used in 1859, are on display. The present St. Stephen's, built in 1870, holds the original stone font from the Old Church. This was recovered from a nearby field.

Many ships were wrecked in the wide bay. The most

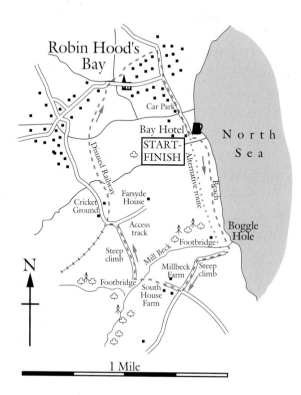

famous rescue occurred in 1881 when Whitby lifeboat was manhandled overland through waist-high snowdrifts to the bay and down the steep bank to save the six crewmen of the brig Visitor.

There are two car parks in Robin Hood's Bay, a large one at the top end of the village, on the former railway station, and the other, smaller one nearer the sea, closer to The Bay Hotel (GR953 048). The hotel is the official finishing point of the Coast to Coast walk.

There is an element of danger in the walk about to be described, as the walk heads across the beach between Robin Hood's Bay and a point known as Boggle Hole. **You must check tide times before starting this walk.**

If you elect to use the former railway station car park, at the top of the village, spare a couple of minutes to read the informative North York Moors National Park notice board. Swing right, heading downhill towards the sea and the lower car park.

Robin Hood's Bay is a delightful coastal resort, and you'll probably be greeted by the sound of gulls as these graceful birds patrol the skies above. Many architecturally pleasing buildings are evident, revealing Victorian prosperity.

There are superb views from the lower car park. Just beyond the car park a poignant plaque reveals the plight of the brig Visitor, on January 18th 1881. The moving citation reveals that due to the violence of the storm no local boat could be launched. The lifeboat from Whitby was brought six miles overland, encountering seven-foot snowdrifts.

Two hundred men cleared the snow and 18 horses pulled the boat towards Robin Hood's Bay. Other teams worked towards them from the seafront. The lifeboat was launched two hours after leaving Whitby, and at the second attempt the crew of the Visitor were saved. The citation concludes: "So that future generations may remember the bravery of Coxswain Henry Freeman and his lifeboat men and the dogged determination of the people of Whitby, Hawsker and Robin Hood's Bay, who were such brave subjects. This memorial was erected in 1981."

Beyond this point the quaint features of the former fishing village soon become apparent. A steep, narrow, winding road leads between the shops, pubs, cottages and museum (a must) downhill to the beach.

Walk down the cobbled slipway onto the shingle beach and veer right. Remember to check the tide times. Allow 45 minutes to reach Boggle Hole. If the tide is against you the Cleveland Way path can be followed south to Boggle Hole.

In addition to the usual attractions associated with a beach walk, there are other things to seek out on this excursion. The cliffs are formed of boulder clay – glacial debris. On the beach, mixed in among the shingle and the rocks are substantial pieces of Shap granite. Shap is in Cumbria, some 70 or so miles away, and these rocks have been transported by Ice Age glaciers. There are some interesting samples to be found, if you look carefully, but remember to watch the tide.

Following an exciting tramp along the beach leave it by turning right into an inlet heading inland. This is Boggle Hole – a boggle being a hob goblin or friendly spirit – (GR955 041).

Proceed uphill following a tarmaced surface, noticing the Youth Hostel which was formerly a mill, below on the right. At this point you've completed one mile.

At the top of the incline turn right at a cross-roads (GR953 037). There are several buildings hereabouts, the first being Millbank Cottage. Continue straight ahead, ignoring Ings Farm and South House Farm. Make towards a large hay barn, then pass through a gateway prior to encountering a steep, twisting descent.

Reaching the bottom, cross Mill Beck using the footbridge then turn left and emerging onto a quiet road where you turn right. Go up the steep hill, accompanied on the right by a well-preserved packhorse trail perhaps connected with the mill (now the Youth Hostel).

Reaching the top of the incline (GR947 043), there are wonderful views of Robin Hood's Bay with the unusually shaped tower of the village church dominant on the skyline. Continue along the road, ignoring a right turn towards Farsyde Stud, but 50m beyond swing 90 degrees right, passing through a wooden gate to follow the Robin Hood's Bay Railway path. There is a signpost, but if you miss it and arrive at the cricket ground, you've gone too far.

Follow the railway track until it is crossed by a main road. At this point leave the railway, veer right, cross the road and enter a lane on the left, signposted Doctor's Surgery, Village Hall. This leads back to the car park, and refreshment at The Bay Hotel.

HARE & HOUNDS

This outing starts with an exciting cliff-top section, following the Cleveland Way. There are some wonderful seaward views on the outward leg.

DISTANCE: 6½ miles
ALLOW: 3½ hours
MAPS: OS Outdoor Leisure Map 27 Eastern area, NE Sheet
PARKING: At the large car park at Robin Hood's Bay or the Hare and Hounds by arrangement (TEL 01947 880453).

Hawsker cum Stainsacre is a joint township in the parish of Whitby, covering about 4,000 acres and with a population of about 1,000.

The village is divided into two parts, High and Low Hawsker, standing four miles south-east of Whitby. The oldest building is Hawsker Hall, built in 1867. The shaft of a cross stands in a small enclosure belonging to the Hall. This is the only evidence remaining of a chapel founded by Aschetine de Hawskegarth in the reign of King Stephen. The present church was erected in 1877 and dedicated to All Saints, as the old chapel had been.

Cock Mill, a secluded place in the woods, is said to have been used for gambling and cock fighting in olden days, as well as a hide-out for home-coming sailors eluding the press gangs. On the cliff, known as Ling Hill, two lighthouses were erected in 1858 by Trinity House, as a guide to mariners approaching Whitby. When both lights were seen, all was well but, should the two lights appear as one, the vessel had to change course or be dashed on the rocks.

Until the 1950s, water was supplied at the village pumps. In those halcyon days Hawsker had a cobbler and a tailor. Both villages had blacksmiths and a local shop with a post office.

It is recommended that you start from the village hall car park in Robin Hood's Bay. This allows refreshment at the Hare and Hounds, approximately half-way round. You may of course prefer to start from the pub, taking refreshment at the end of the outing. Should you follow the latter option, prior permission must be obtained for car parking at the pub. The walk to be described sets out from Robin Hood's Bay station car park.

Leave the car park walking away from the former railway buildings and cross the main road to enter Mount

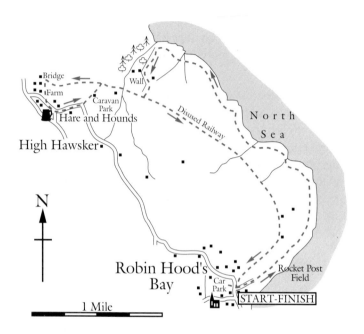

Pleasant North. At the far end of this street follow the Cleveland Way sign.

Initially the way is duckboarded and instantly the first of many superb views across the bay is presented. Pass through a gate to enter an area known as Rocket Post Field, then swing right.

A rocket post once stood in this field. It was used by coastguards as a practice target for rescuing the crews of ships in distress. A rocket secured to a rope was fixed at the post, which simulated a ship's mast, then life saving equipment was attached. The post was erected in 1923 and was in use until 1980 when the use of helicopters rendered it obsolete. An original rocket post can be seen at Ravenscar on land owned by the National Trust.

The walk continues along the cliff top footpath where magnificent scenery abounds. Look for the white painted coastguard lookout station away to your left. The route needs no further description until a recently constructed stone path is encountered and a signpost indicates the National Trust Centenary Path. At this point leave the coastal path, swinging 90 degrees left. Cross the stile and follow the wall steeply uphill, to arrive at the former railway track. Turn right and walk along the track until you arrive at a bridge. At this point leave the track and ascend the bank to a stile on the right.

Cross the bridge and follow the lane, soon passing through a farm prior to arriving at the main road. Veer left to the Hare and Hounds (GR927 075).

After refreshments leave the pub, turning right along the road. At a junction turn left, then after leaving the confines of High Hawsker leave the road at a point where it bends significantly and enters an access road to a caravan park.

Immediately beyond the first set of caravans, the road crosses the railway track used earlier and you turn right. The ensuing two miles to Robin Hood's Bay following the railway track covers delightful coastal scenery.

A waymarked gate near houses marks the end of the railway section. From the gate turn left and re-enter Mount Pleasant North en-route to the car park beyond.

WHITE SWAN

P I C K E R I N G

Considering this walk starts from a large town, it is surprising how soon you'll be walking in open countryside and forests. Much to see and enjoy en route.

DISTANCE: 5 miles
ALLOW: 3 hours
MAP: OS Outdoor Leisure Map 27 Eastern area, SE Sheet
PARKING: Car park at junction of A169/170. Pub telephone 01751 472288.

Pickering is a small, friendly market town, situated at the southern end of the North York Moors National Park. The town is said to take its name from a ring being found inside a pike caught in water, close to the town. In years gone by the town celebrated many annual local customs and events. On Shrove Tuesday the Pancake Bell was rung at eleven o'clock signalling the closure of schools and business for the day. In early July all church Sunday schools congregated in the market place for the annual rail outing to Scarborough. Local farmers gathered in November for the 'The Hirings' when labour required for the coming year was hired at the Michaelmas Fair.

The site of the old cattle market in Eastgate has become a Tourist Information Centre and provides ample parking. The 15th century parish church of St. Peter and St. Paul contains fine medieval wall frescoes. The Beck Isle Museum was formerly the home of William Marshall, author of Rural Economy of Yorkshire. The museum holds many examples of local crafts, machinery and the rural way of life on the North York Moors. North of the town are the remains of a very fine castle still displaying evidence of a moat, bridge towers and dungeons.

This walk crosses the railway line several times. Extra vigilance, responsible behaviour and caution are called for.

The walk starts from the large car park close to the junction of the A169/A170. Leave the car park and proceed uphill along the Whitby road, passing Pickering County Infants' School on the right. Soon after the school you'll pass the amusingly named Hat Box Lane.

Continue in the same direction eventually passing a sheltered housing complex on

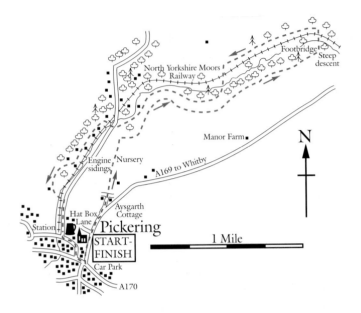

your left. Immediately after this, swing left into Love
Lane (GR802 844) alongside Aysgarth Cottage
(signpost), then proceed in a straight line passing
through a modern housing estate. Cross a lane
(signposted) and continue in the same direction.

A few yards further on ignore the right turn indicated
but continue straight ahead, passing through a nursery to
arrive at a stile. From the stile continue straight across a
cultivated field, making towards Lowther Wood. On
reaching the boundary of the wood DON'T pass through
the gate, instead veer right to follow the boundary fence
for a mile. Along the way several stiles are negotiated,
although you should ignore the one situated at an angle

in the boundary fence which gives access to the wood.

Continue along the field, with the fence to your left. The wood's name changes from Lowther to Featherhaugh and then to Little Park Wood, although you'll be unaware of the changes.

Eventually a ladder stile is encountered and crossed to enter the woodland (GR823 858). Proceed straight on, walking along a well-defined track to arrive at a white marker post. Turn left, downhill to eventually join a broad track. Cross this track then follow a narrow path, leading to and crossing a footbridge to arrive at the railway.

Cross the railway then turn left, following a broad track alongside the railway to your left. You are now walking through Pickering Woods, a conifer plantation belonging to the Duchy of Lancaster. After leaving the plantation via a gate, turn left at an obvious junction, then after 50m swing left once more and re-cross the railway track.

Head towards and cross over the footbridge, (GR814 857) veering right across the field and then soon walking alongside a beck. Keep in close contact with the fence to your left, then when a stile is reached, hop over it and veer right now walking in woodland with the fence to your right. Notice the North Yorkshire Moors Railway depot away to the right.

A stile leads you out of the wood, following a clear path passing between a shed and a house. Beyond these, at the end of the driveway, swing right to cross the road, then a footbridge near Bridge Cottage. Pass in front of a row of tidy cottages and cross the railway again. Then, after passing the last cottage, swing left through a gate to walk alongside some allotments. Pass a rather quaint cottage, noticing all the memorabilia. Pickering Castle is situated on a pronounced mound away to the left.

A short way beyond the house at an obvious bend, leave the track and pass through a heavily fortified gate. Cross the field, veering slightly left to locate a well-concealed stone step stile, close to a wall corner. Cross this to follow a delightful beck-side footpath to arrive at The Vale of Pickering Scout hut. Turn left and re-cross the railway, then swing right and walk into the centre of Pickering. The White Swan is situated midway along the main street, on the left.

The car park where the walk started lies a short distance beyond The White Swan, following the main street.

THE CROWN

The spectacular moorland villages of Hutton-le-Hole and Lastingham are high spots of this walk. Allow sufficient time to explore the ancient crypt church of St Mary's, Lastingham.

DISTANCE: 4 miles
ALLOW: 2¹/₂ hours
MAP: OS Outdoor Leisure Map 26. North York Moors Western Area SW Sheet
PARKING: Large public car park

Hutton-le-Hole is a beautiful village resting several miles to the NE of Kirkbymoorside in the North York Moors National Park. Flowing through the village is Hutton Beck, which divides the traditional stone cottages, sprinkled around a large central green. Moorland sheep fastidiously tend the green, keeping it closely cropped throughout the year.

The area has been occupied since prehistoric times. Those wishing to learn more about the history of Hutton and the surrounding area should visit the Ryedale Folk Museum in the village.

The common land rights are administered by the Court Leet of the Manor of Spaunton, which remains responsible for the management of the adjoining moorland and Hutton Common. This ancient custom still affects village life. A small 'fine' (rent) to a maximum of £2 is levied for private enclosure of commonland, including a fenced garden in front of a house. The Court Leet is mentioned in the Danby notes (p71) and dates from the Middle Ages. Recently, when a new Lord of the Manor inherited the title, he and numerous common rights' holders 'walked the bounds' navigating their way through knee-high heather and waist-deep streams. The circuit took two days to complete.

The walk begins from the main car park in Hutton-le-Hole (GR705 903) veering left and soon after left again at the junction opposite the gift shop. Walk through the picturesque village, passing the Crown pub (meals are available 12-2.30pm and 7-9pm – tel 01751 417343) and the Ryedale Folk Museum. Continue past the telephone box and St. Chad's Church, then opposite the village hall swing left, passing through a signposted gate.

Beyond the gate a zigzag path leads out into fields to the rear of the church. Continue in a straight line across several fields linked by stiles, to arrive at a footbridge which spans the delightfully named Fairy Call Beck (GR711 903). A clear forest path leads away from the bridge, rising steadily to arrive at the forest exit gate. From the gate continue ahead for a short way to arrive at a road where you turn right.

Continue along the road, ignoring the access track on the left leading to Bainwood, until the road descends and approaches a bridge. Just prior to the bridge, leave the road, swinging left as indicated by the signpost (GR722 904). The track leads on to the moorland after passing through a gate. After 100m the path divides and you follow the right fork, accompanying first a wall then a fence to your right.

Soon after follow a signpost pointing diagonally left and aim for the wall corner some way ahead. The curiously named Camomile Farm stands across the way on the right. From the wall angle keep close to the the wall as it descends and ascends steeply to a signpost and a welcoming seat (GR729 909).

After a brief stop, continue downhill in the direction the seat faces to the rather special village of Lastingham. From the junction at the bottom of the hill the walk will eventually veer left, but a detour to the right is strongly recommended as this takes you to the Blacksmith's Arms.

The Blacksmith's Arms hasn't altered significantly since the late 18th century when it was kept by the curate's wife, with the intention to raise £20 per year towards the upkeep of their 13 children. The colourful curate, the Rev. Jeremiah Carter appeared before his superiors for playing a musical instrument and dancing in the pub on the Sabbath. He explained that his parishioners had to

travel many miles across the moors to attend services and needed refreshments before returning home. He maintained that in order to direct them from too much liquor and 'bad' conversation, he would play his fiddle and would not refuse the young folk if they wished to dance. The archdeacon was apparently satisfied with his explanation.

Another important attraction is St. Mary's church where a plaque outside the church reveals: "The ancient crypt church of St. Mary of Lastingham, the sign of St. Cedd. Built in 1078 on the site of a Celtic monastery." Inside the church there's a rather special feature – an 11th century crypt. The church and the crypt are open to the public during daylight hours.

Resuming the walk from where you first entered the village, walk along the lane, passing the telephone box and the Wesleyan chapel on the left. Just beyond a cottage bearing a datestone 1783, veer right crossing Jackson Bridge. The bridge was erected as a memorial to John Jackson, RA in 1865. The bridge also displays a plate Y.N.R. 626. This is the bridge maintenance number, as documented by the former Yorkshire North Riding Highways Department.

Beyond the bridge towards the end of the lane, turn right at a signpost up an incline. Notice the sapling planted in September 1990 to commemorate the 75th anniversary of the Women's Institute.

The ascent is quite steep, but the effort is rewarded with wonderful retrospective views of Lastingham. Emerging onto a road (GR729 899), cross over making towards the village of Spaunton, a small village standing some

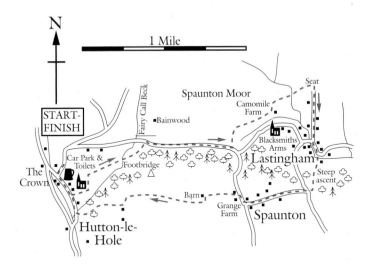

600ft (183m) above sea level.

The Manor House at the eastern end of the village has been rebuilt several times. The Court Leet still sits on the first Thursday in October. A pinder and 12 jury men are sworn in and impose fines on people who have illegally encroached onto the manor's common land. The pinfold is at the western end of the village, close to the remains of the former chapel. Towards the end of 1943, an RAF bomber crashed on the village, demolishing the blacksmith's shop and a cottage. The tenant of Manor Farm was killed by the force of the exploding bombs as he went to investigate.

The village has few amenities, but it has retained a Victorian letter box and before leaving Spaunton you will notice a lintel datestone of 1695 incorporated into Woodman's Cottage.

Continue through the village swinging right at the junction then left to enter Grange Farm (GR723 899). Waymarkers point the way through and beyond the farm so route finding problems shouldn't arise. Arriving at a signpost close to some farm outbuildings, observe the splendid panoramic views of Blakey Ridge and Spaunton Moors, before continuing left as directed. After 100m turn right, entering an enclosed track with a wire fence to the left and a stone wall on the right (GR718 898).

Eventually the rooftops of Hutton-le-Hole appear below. Keep following the same track which again swings left then after 20m turn right to a downhill track. After a short distance cross over a stile, then after only 10m leave the track via another stile on the right.

From this descend into Hutton-le-Hole and refreshments at The Crown, crossing a section which is often wet and muddy. A stream close to the road is useful for boot washing. At the road turn right and go through the village.

Most of the houses in Hutton-le-Hole were built between 1650-1750 on the site formerly occupied by Anglo-Saxons. Strong connections with the Quaker movement developed in the village and a meeting house was erected in 1698. During the ensuing 200 years Methodism became popular, and by 1860 there were two Methodist and Congregational chapels. The present Anglican church was built in 1934.

SALTERSGATE INN

A pub brimming with legend, the wild expanse of Levisham moor and the Hole of Horcum all provide a walk full of potential.

DISTANCE: 4¹/₂ miles
ALLOW: 2¹/₂ – 3 hours
MAP: OS Outdoor Leisure Map 27. North York Moors Eastern Area SE Sheet
PARKING: Either at the pub (Tel 01751 460237) or large car park alongside A171.

This walk can be undertaken from the Saltersgate Inn, at the foot of Saltersgate Bank. But in order to minimise walking along an often busy road, it's suggested that you start from the large free car park alongside the A171 road overlooking the spectacular Hole of Horcum.

The fire, blazing in the highly burnished Pickering-made cast iron range in the Saltersgate Inn (GR852 944), has burned uninterrupted for 200 years, according to legend. Ever since 1796, when a group of smugglers are reputed to have murdered a Customs and Excise officer and buried his body underneath the hearth stone, the fire has continued to blaze.

To ensure the hearthstone was never lifted the murderers made up and embellished a tale involving the Devil. They claimed the Devil burst into the inn one night threatening everyone with damnation. To mollify him, customers offered him a seat close to the fire, subsequently pushing him onto the fire. The felons stressed that should the fire ever go out the Devil would reappear and plague the neighbourhood.

The surrounding area has other strong connections with the Devil. The Hole of Horcum is reputed to have been created by the Devil's endeavours. The sharp bend on the A171 road close to the inn, is known as the Devil's Elbow. The inn's sign still displays the Devil's face within the flickering fire.

Another interesting feature at the Saltersgate Inn is the tiller of the 62-year-old fishing smack Helga Maria, in which the Whitby fisherman Jack Lammiman sailed to the Arctic Circle in 1991. This voyage was in defiance of a Department of Transport order confining him to port. Lammiman made the 2,300 mile voyage in honour of Whitby whaling skippers William Scoresby, senior and junior.

From the car park, cross the road carefully then turn right. At once the imagination is stirred by the dramatic landscape displayed below. It is pleasing to know in advance that the final part of this outing threads its way through that landscape, a treat to savour for later in the day! As the road tilts steeply downhill and bends sharply at the Devil's Elbow, veer off on the left, towards a wide gate. Ignore the ladder stile – that will be negotiated at the end of the walk.

Pass through the gate which gives access onto the moorland. A few paces along the wide vehicle track, an attractive metal plaque (the first of many) discloses terms and conditions for access to Levisham Moor. These must be strictly observed.

The track unfurls across the moor and description isn't necessary. About a mile along the way you pass another plaque mounted onto a rock to your right. This relates to an ancient earthworks and a ditch known as Cross Dyke.

It reads: "Large ditch with two banks was constructed 2,000 years ago, probably to mark the territory of a pastoral people. Behind you the earthworks on the near horizon are part of a fortified farmstead built at a similar date."

After about an hour's walking and 2¼ miles, you arrive at a cross-roads and a signpost near Dundale Pond.

A plaque here discloses: "This small valley was given to the monks of Malton Priory in 1230, as pasture for their sheep, cattle and horses. Dundale Pond was probably made at this time as a place for their stock to drink."

From the cross-roads turn left towards Dundale Griff. After a short distance and unusually, in the middle of a moor, you walk alongside a significant section of deciduous woodland,

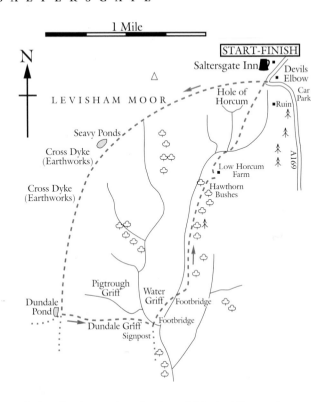

consisting in the main of oak and birch. The path gradually descends and passes two tributary valleys, Pigtrough Griff and Water Griff. The former relates to the earlier mentioned oak trees, for in medieval times pigs reared on monastic estates were fed on acorns.

Shortly after passing these tributaries, the track curves to the right and a signpost instructs you to swing left to Saltersgate. Cross over two footbridges then veer left, ignoring the gate directly ahead.

The route briefly accompanies Horcum Dyke, a sparkling moorland stream, and soon arrives at a stile where a wondrous view is presented. A secret valley unfurls before you. When I visited here in February 1996, it was cloaked with glistening snow. It was an absolutely stunning setting which I shall never forget.

Because of the snow the footpath was indiscernable, so I followed a line close to the wall and fence on my right to an angle in the fence then I trudged across the field in the same direction as before to pass between some hawthorn bushes. Eventually the track leads to the derelict Low Horcum Farm.

Low Horcum farm was built in 1811 and inhabited until 1966. This ruin and boundary wall are all that remain. At one time two farms occupied the Hole of Horcum, but High Horcum Farmstead about 800m NE was demolished mainly by high winds, in January 1963. The restoration of Low Horcum was completed in 1986 by the Youth Project (Age Concern) for the national park.

If you approach the farm with caution you might be fortunate and see some deer. Continue from the farm following the same line as before and pass through a gate some 300m beyond the farm in a depression.

Climb up a steep incline to arrive at a ladder stile. Cross this veering right for a short distance to the car park. If your vehicle is at the Saltersgate Inn, turn left down the road. Whichever route you've selected, now's the time for a reward at the Saltersgate Inn.

HORSESHOE INN

L E V I S H A M

This walk visits two superb viewpoints, at Skelton Tower and Surprise View, both offering glorious panoramas of Newton Dale.

Not to be undertaken in misty conditions

DISTANCE: 4 miles
ALLOW: 2¹/₂ hours
MAP: OS Outdoor Leisure Map 27 North York Moors Eastern Area SE Sheet
PARKING: Around village green or at Horseshoe Inn by arrangement (Tel 01751 460240).

A quiet backwater accurately describes Levisham, although the village has a church (St. John the Baptist), Levisham Hall and a thriving inn, the Horseshoe. The village is linked to the A169 via Lockton by a narrow, winding road which contains substantial gradients. It will be easy to be shut out or in, when snow falls around Levisham.

Commence the walk following Limpsey Gate Lane which passes to the right side of the Horseshoe Inn past a cottage bearing an 1860 datestone. Soon the tiny, underground Levisham Reservoir is encountered on the left. Keep on treading the same route to a gate which gives access onto Levisham Moor (GR830 917).

Pass through the gate and continue to follow the same line as before, signposted Saltersgate.

A metal plaque sited just beyond the gate declares: "Levisham Estate. This land is owned by the National Park Committee and you are welcome to walk here. Please note that vehicles,

metal detectors, guns, fires and tents are not allowed on the moor. We would be grateful if you would close gates and keep dogs on a lead."

The path descends steadily and arrives at a major cross-roads at a signpost.

Note: Take extra care between this point and Skelton Tower. Follow the indication to 'the station' (this being several miles away and not encountered on this outing), walking alongside then beyond the pond. The path is intermittent through the heather, the general line being westwards. The path steadily rises and eventually merges with a wall to your left, arriving close to an angle in the wall (GR824 919). From the angle veer away to the right, now heading north-westerly away from the wall to follow a well-defined green track.

The way forward is now easy to follow and soon arrives at an obvious right-hand curve. Keep striding confidently on as the track descends. The next point of interest is

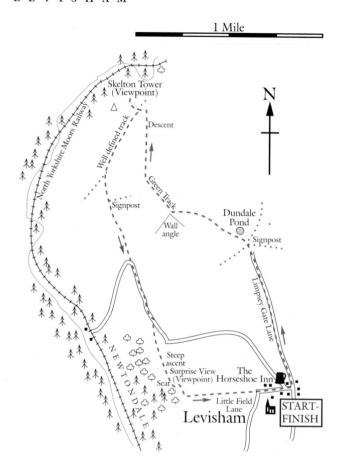

already in view – Skelton Tower, a square-shaped, ruined
building built by the Rev. Robert Skelton, curate of
Levisham between 1814-19. The two-storeyed, castellated
building incorporating superb arched windows was
formerly a shooting lodge (GR820 928).

The views of Newtondale and the Pickering-Grosmont railway 250ft (76m) below are quite staggering and the short detour is more than justified.

From the tower retrace your steps about 200m to a broad track crossed earlier and swing right where a waymarker confirms your route. A little farther on a new (1996) three-pronged signpost is encountered. Continue in the same direction as before, eventually emerging onto a road at a sharp bend where you veer left.

Ignore the invitations to turn left then right soon afterwards, but when a road sign indicating a 20% gradient is encountered leave the road on the right, then turn slightly left, deliberately avoiding a gate.

Continue with the boundary on your right side to arrive at a signpost. Head towards "the village" which involves a stiff climb. A seat has been thoughtfully installed at the top (GR824 906) and is known locally as Surprise View.

Enjoy the view of Levisham railway station and the railway track wriggling along the valley. Directly across the valley is the village of Newton-on-Rawcliffe.

Continue along the narrow, high-level path which soon swings 90 degrees right before rising steadily to arrive at a stile. Cross this then accompany the wall on the left across several arable fields – please walk in single file.

The roof tops of Levisham are now in view and soon the fields are left to join Little Field Lane where you turn left. The lane leads past the former school building, to emerge close to the church of St. John the Baptist and Levisham Hall. The Horseshoe Inn is then only a minute's walk.

THE HART

Fantastic sea views by treading sections of the Cleveland Way ensure a pleasant half-day's outing with lots of interest.

DISTANCE: 6¼ miles
ALLOW: 3½-4 hours
MAPS: OS Outdoor Leisure Map 27 North York Moors Eastern Area NE Sheet
PARKING: Choice of two, one at the bottom of Lythe Bank, at the western end of the village, the other is nearer the Hart close to the bridge at East Row.

The picturesque village of Sandsend nestles on the coastline at the foot of Lythe Bank, three miles north-west of Whitby. The village is divided into two communities, East and West Rows.

This attractive resort once had a thriving alum industry dating from the 17th century, with hundreds of men employed at the Sandsend works. When the mines closed in 1871 another industry flourished, producing a quick setting cement capable of repairing a sea wall between tides. The product was Sandsend Roman Cement, made from stones known as 'dogger stones' discarded as being useless in times of alum production. A mill formerly used for grinding corn in East Row was converted to cement grinding and the mill building remains, now known as Mill Cottage, close to East Row car park. The conical kiln, where dogger stones were burnt prior to grinding, is at the rear of Mill Cottage.

Before the railway closed in 1958 the railway from Whitby to Loftus was a prominent feature with tall viaducts

and the line running on a shelf on the hillside behind the houses. Now the former railway track is popular with walkers and the surrounding area has become a haven for wildlife.

West Row, with its delightful small cottages and St. Mary's chapel, presents a very peaceful scene and is particularly attractive when the daffodils are in bloom. The village also has distant associations with Indian hierarchy in the form of the Maharajah Duleep Singh. I'm indebted to Peter Walker for the following tale:

The Maharajah was exiled from India in 1849 and leased nearby Mulgrave Castle for four years, while the Marquis of Normanby was in London. Together with two Indians and six gamekeepers dressed in red uniforms, the Maharajah went hawking on the moors wearing oriental

dress. What a splendid sight they must have been.

At that time there wasn't a road along the coast between Sandsend and Whitby, so he financed its construction. This was done, it's said, because his elephants had difficulty walking along the sandy beach. Fact or fiction? We'll never know.

The walk can start from either of two village car parks. One is at the bottom of Lythe Bank, at the western end of the village. This has toilets and is pay and display. The other is nearer the Hart (TEL 01947 893304 – bar meals in high season), close to the bridge at East Row.

From East Row walk along the seafront towards the large car park previously mentioned. Pass through the car park and climb the 50 steps to emerge close to the former Sandsend railway station. Turn right, walking along the railway track, high above the sea.

A left turn which isn't obvious is looming up, so watch out for the post displaying Trail 7 and Walk 17. Turn left about 100m beyond this. A brick wall on your right, constructed to prevent further cliff erosion, confirms the spot. From there climb a grassy bank, cross a stile and proceed straight ahead, noticing an old stone drainage channel. Keep rising, passing through some bushes and head across the field towards Deepgrove Farm (GR853 137).

Arriving at the farm turn right, signposted Kettleness. Proceed carefully across several fields, prior to descending to and ascending from a wooded dell known as Overdale. A stile gives access into a ploughed field where you turn slightly left, keeping to the boundary.

After a short way a wide gap in the hedge and a stile appear. At this point swing left through the gap. Overdale Farm is across the field on the left. From the gap walk in a straight line, along the edge of the fields, eventually merging with a road. Turn right, en-route to the village of Goldsborough.

Continue past the first building – the Fox and Hounds with its red pantile roof – and a signpost to Kettleness.

After 200m swing right just beyond the main farm buildings to pass through a farmyard to a stile. Continue ahead (often muddy here) to an upright marker post. From the post veer left across a field making towards a pronounced mound in the distance, to the left of a telegraph pole (GR835 152).

This mound was the site of Goldsborough Roman Signal Station. The information board relates: "About 368A.D., a series of signal stations were built along the coast between Flamborough Head and the River Tees. These were used to provide the Roman garrisons with an early warning of Scottish or Saxon raiders. Goldsborough signal station is one of five remaining examples of this defensive system."

The walk continues by crossing the stile close to the information board, then heading diagonally right across the field towards another stile. This is located to the right of a large, well preserved building which has an decoratively tiled roof. Beyond this, a second stile leads onto the road which is followed into the village of Kettleness, passing the substantial former railway station en-route (GR831 156).

A wonderful view of Runswick Bay soon appears and the industrialised activity is Boulby potash mine. Proceed towards the cliff top (just beyond a vegetable garden) and swing hard right by a Cleveland Way sign.

This delightful coastal path is followed unerringly to Sandsend. It's well waymarked and route finding shouldn't be a problem. Along the way you'll observe both entrances to Sandsend railway tunnel, which is about 3/4 mile (1.2km) long. The first tunnel entrance

isn't obvious, situated some 100m away from the
footpath, but the next is unmistakable at the foot of some
extremely steep steps (GR854 142).

*Another interesting feature which should be apparent as you
follow the coastal path is the alum excavations. These
enormous excavations claimed more of the original coastline
than sea erosion and are particularly conspicuous from a
signpost junction of the Cleveland Way and Lythe Walk 17.*

The walk concludes with superb views across Sandsend
Bay with Whitby Abbey prominent in the distance.

COD AND LOBSTER

S T A I T H E S

Staithes lies at the foot of a steep hill, between cliffs a few miles north of Whitby. Its cobbled streets and back alleys evoke an old world charm. The village's most recent acquisition is the new school, in stark contrast to the old one – an austere Victorian building which opened in 1878. The east coast weather is often severe, the school log of 1897 indicating that great storms of wind "blew in the windows and destroyed the perimeter wall". Older boys would go fishing with their fathers during the spring and summer, younger children went to the woods to collect ash branches for making crab pots. Children of miners were particularly poor and many were not able to afford school fees.

Numbers of children attending the school fell dramatically during the 1920s, with the closure of the ironstone mines. Many families moved to Middlesbrough to find alternative employment.

Start this sea-sprinkled walk from the large pay and display car park at the top of the hill, high above the harbour. Proceed downhill to the former fishing village.

Pass the school, then continue downhill noticing the Bethal Chapel, Primitive Methodist Chapel (1880) and, close to the seafront, the Mission Church of St. Peter the Fisherman. After inspecting the seafront, head into Church Street, a steep, narrow street, which soon peters out and continues steeply as a rough, uneven track. Cleveland Way signs confirm the way.

Reaching the top of the incline, the path levels out and continues straight ahead, passing a farm on the right, (GR784 187) before unfurling as a superb coastal path. The path twists, rises and falls and eventually crosses a field towards Port Mulgrave – once an ironstone mining centre. Throughout there are superb views of the coast and sea, making this a walk never to be forgotten.

Enter Port Mulgrave via a gate at the far right hand

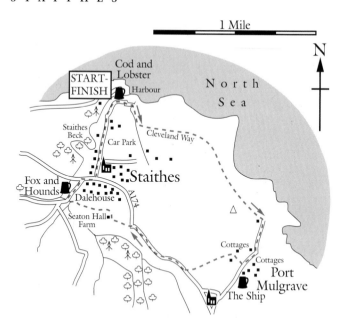

corner of the field, then continue along the road. The rows of cottages were originally constructed to house the miners and their families. Close to a signpost to Rosedale Lane, it's worth turning off the road on the left to read the information board associated with the Port Mulgrave Ironstone Mine. Far below the board the scant remains of the harbour will be observed.

Ironstone mining began in 1855. The following year work commenced on the construction of the harbour at a cost of £45,000. Entrance to the mine was at the foot of the cliffs. Gantries led out from the mine on which tubs ran, tipping ore into a succession of bunkers. The ore was unloaded from the bunkers directly onto waiting ships. The operation continued until 1917, when operations were gradually scaled down. A new owner, trading as the Grinkle Mine, took over but by 1921 was in difficulty because of coal strikes during the depression. These actions were significant factors in the ultimate closure of the mines.

The walk continues along the road, then swings right on reaching the telephone box. Port Mulgrave's public house, The Ship, is 500m beyond this junction. Pass the Anchorage (a strange name for a building at the top of the cliffs) then continue through a waymarked gate. After 20m swing left, then walk in a direct line, eventually descending to a main road (A174) where you turn right.

Walk alongside the road for approximately 800m, until the road bends sharply right. At that point cross over and enter a farm access track at a signpost (GR784 177). Walk along the track then immediately before reaching the farm buildings, hop over a stile on the right. Make towards some modern houses and locate another stile and follow the sign to Dalehouse. The way crosses several fields in a straight line from the stile, eventually descending into the hamlet of Dalehouse (GR 777 180), complete with its appealing looking public house – the Fox and Hounds. Dropping down from the fields onto the road, swing right (unless calling at the pub) to follow a steep incline to its junction with the busy A174 road. From this point bear right, cross over and enter Staithes Lane where there's a police station on the corner.

This leads past the Roman Catholic church, to the car park. Now make your way down the hill to the harbour for refreshments at the Cod and Lobster (TEL 01947 840295).

MILBURN ARMS

ROSEDALE ABBEY

An outing full of potential in beautiful Rosedale. Save this one for a fine day.

DISTANCE: 3½ miles
ALLOW: 2 hours
MAP: OS Outdoor Leisure Map 26 North York Moors Western Area SW Sheet.
PARKING: Free alongside Milburn Arms (TEL 01751 417312.)

Nestling in one of the region's best-known and visited valleys, Rosedale Abbey is to the north-west of Pickering and reached via the A170. Not much is left of the abbey but the scant remains, a stone's throw from the Milburn Arms, can still be visited. The Milburn Arms is a superb pub – an oasis in a remote location. A full range of meals and sandwiches are avaliable, but check availability out of the peak season.

From the pretty, attractively named village of Rosedale Abbey, start by leaving the free car park alongside the Milburn Arms and turning left. Continue up the road, away from the village, soon passing a cottage appropriately named Rosedale and then a converted chapel.

Opposite the entrance to Haygate Farm cross a ladder stile (GR729 964). Head directly ahead across the field to another stile which requires a little care on descending. Head across the next field, veering slightly left and through a gate, then swing right close by a waymark fixed to a

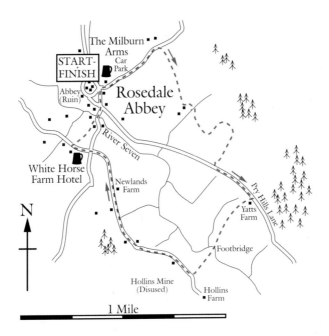

telegraph pole. Approaching Grange Farm, pass to the left of a wooden barn which is straight ahead, then at once turn right and left through gates. Continue walking close to the wall on the right. At the second gate a signpost points the way left, uphill towards a huge ladder stile.

Cross this, veering left to follow the wall on your left, heading towards a waymark painted on an oak tree. Beyond this, after hopping over a stile, is a signpost. From the stile (GR 735 935) swing right and down the field to a gate which gives access to a road where you turn left.

Follow the road for a short way to Yatts Farm on the right. Immediately before the farm buildings go right, and follow directions indicated by an abundance of 'home made' signs. These invite you to follow the field edge to your right side, leading to a footbridge across the river Seven. Cross the bridge, then continue straight ahead, walking uphill towards a gate. Emerging onto a minor road, swing right (GR733 946).

Before moving off notice the mounds in the fields above. These are the spoil heaps associated with Hollins Mine, where ironstone was mined from 1856 and throughout the second half of the 19th century. At first the ore was taken out of the valley on wagons, but due to the rapidly deteriorating roadways a railway was constructed. The line

*crossed the moors from the north, terminating high above
Rosedale Abbey. A steam driven engine powered wagons
uphill from the mine to the railway. As a result a
landowner demanded a 50ft (15m) chimney should be
erected to prevent the smoke from affecting his grouse. This
was the famous Rosedale Chimney, a landmark for years
until its demolition in 1972.*

Proceed along the lane soon passing Holly Cottage and
its pottery studio. Three substantial houses are
encountered en-route to Newlands Farm. The minor road
merges with the farm track, but the direction is
unchanged. Soon after you arrive at the White Horse
Farm Hotel (GR724 955). From here cross the road to a
dead end road, signposted Thorgill only. There's a
concealed stile on the right, opposite Red House Golf
Club; hop over this to descend through the field towards
the village of Rosedale Abbey, which should be in sight.

Keep close to the hedge on your right and cross a stile
close to a house. Descend the steps, walk through a
garden, then swing left to arrive back in the village of
Rosedale Abbey.

DUKE OF WELLINGTON

DANBY

The moorland section between Ainthorpe and Little Fryup Dale needs careful navigation but that little extra care will ensure an enjoyable circuit.

DISTANCE: 4 miles
ALLOW: 2 hours
MAP: OS Outdoor Leisure Map 26 North York Moors Western Area NW sheet
PARKING: National Park Moors Centre, Danby Lodge, or roadside close to pub (Tel 01287 660351)

Danby was founded by Danish settlers and the parish church stands in the middle of the dale close to the site of the original village. It is likely that the church was built of stone taken from the old fortress at Castleton. The watermill has recently been restored and stoneground flour is once more for sale. In the early 1900s the miller, Mr Petlar charged one penny a stone for grinding.

Only four miles long much of the way roadwalking, this walk is packed with interesting features. There are two pretty villages, the Moors Centre, a ruined castle and a superb pack horse bridge – Duck Bridge. The route also includes a wondrous moorland section, leading into Little Fryup Dale – a spectacularly beautiful "hidden" valley.

The walk could be started from either Danby and Ainthorpe, but for ease of parking the outing is described from the Moors Centre car park (GR717 084).

Leave the car park turning right to walk along the road. Beyond the left hand bend the road (Lodge Lane) rises steeply and you'll soon notice a superb triple-arched barn on the right, associated with Danby Lodge Farm. Continue along the road to Danby which is dominated by its red, pantile rooftops. A row of tidy bungalows is encountered along Lodge Lane.

After passing the village post office you reach the Duke of Wellington, a former 18th century coaching inn. The pub is at the road junction where you turn left (GR708 087), making towards the next village – Ainthorpe. Pass the village hall, noticing the ship's wheel gate at No. 15 Dale End. The Methodist church, erected in 1811 and rebuilt 90 years later, is on the right.

The entrance to Danby railway station is reached a short way before the track is crossed by the road bridge. Danby Water Mill, also known as Esk Mill, is on the right. Cross the river Esk using the bridge bearing a Highways Department identification plate YNR 310

D A N B Y

(Yorkshire North Riding).

At a junction swing left into Brook Lane and the village of Ainthorpe, where another refreshment stop could be made at the Fox and Hounds, the oldest pub in the area dating back to 1555. Climbing steadily out of the village, take advantage of the superb views to your right.

Leave the road on the right, about 75m beyond the tennis courts (signpost), then thread your way through a small area of gorse bushes, to arrive at a gate (GR707 075) which leads to the moorland. A well-defined path leads steeply from the gate and offers superb retrospective views of Danby and the surrounding area. **Careful navigation is required during the ensuing mile towards Little Fryup Dale.**

From the gate the track rises and you should leave it on the left after 400m (GR707 069), 50m before reaching a pile of stones, to follow a faint, narrow track eastwards across the moor. If you reach an upright boundary stone on your right, you've gone too far. Eventually the path reaches a facing wall and veers right. Soon after, Little Fryup Dale and a splendid vista which includes the unmistakable shape of Round Hill come into view. .

A short descent brings you to a cattle grid alongside Crossley Gate Farm (GR717 066). At that point swing left to continue along the road.

After half a mile you reach Danby Castle Farm and the commanding ruins of Danby Castle. The castle was originally built in the 14th century by William, Lord Latimer, as a fortified palace. The building consisted of a central courtyard with towers at each corner. Catherine

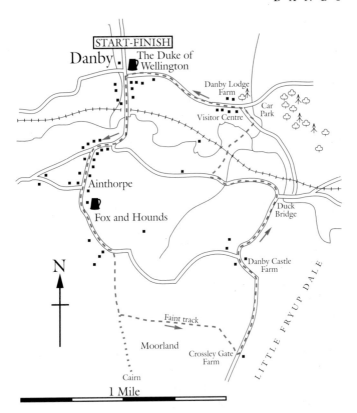

Parr, the sixth wife of Henry VIII, married John, Lord Latimer who lived at Danby Castle.

Danby Castle contains an old chest holding the documents of the Danby Court Leet and Baron. This continues to administer rights of way and common lands in the parish of Danby. In 1977 many existing Courts Leet had their jurisdictions curtailed but 31 were allowed to continue in

*England and Wales. Five of these, including Danby, are
within the North York Moors area, and each undertakes its
function very seriously.*

A short way beyond the castle bear right at a junction
and continue along the road. The Moors Visitor Centre
is in view again. Pass the entrance to Castle Houses –
probably built with stone plundered from the original
castle.

*The final point of interest soon comes into view. This is the
magnificent pack horse bridge known as Duck Bridge, an
ancient monument bearing a badly eroded coat of arms,
possibly that of the Latimer family. Duck Bridge is
sometimes referred to as Dux Bridge or Dukes Bridge, but
these names are incorrect. The bridge spans the Esk and
was originally constructed in 1345 when it was known as
Castle Bridge. Following severe flood damage during the
18th century the bridge was restored by a local builder
George Duck.*

From Duck Bridge continue along the road to a stile on
the right where a signpost indicates Danby Lodge (GR
715 079). Go over the stile and directly ahead, crossing
the railway then the River Esk en-route to the Moors
Centre and the conclusion of the walk.

HORSESHOE HOTEL

E G T O N   B R I D G E

This walk takes in the picturesque village of Egton Bridge, Beggar's Bridge and passes through the delightful Arncliff Woods.

DISTANCE: 3¹/₂ miles
ALLOW: 2¹/₄ hours
MAP: OS Outdoor Leisure Map 27, North York Moors, Eastern Area NE sheet
PARKING: Car park alongside St Hedda's Church.

The tidy, picturesque village of Egton Bridge in Eskdale contains two special attractions – the new road bridge and St Hedda's Church – as well as being host on the first Tuesday in August to the 200-year-old Egton Bridge Gooseberry Show.

In 1993 the bridge replaced a 'temporary' construction erected in 1930. It was built by a stonemason from nearby Sleights, Tom Atkinson, and his ten-man team who completed the job in just 17 weeks.

The walk starts from the free car park next to St Hedda's Church at Egton Bridge. An alternative would be to seek permission from the proprietors at the Horseshoe Hotel (TEL 01947 85245).

Leave the car park, turning right then right again after the church. Proceed along the road, passing the quaintly-named Stepping Stones cottage on the left. A pretty section of the River Esk follows, its banks adorned with wild garlic and primroses in spring.

Leaving the village, continue along

the road passing under a railway bridge and by Broom House Farm. Almost at once, as the road goes steeply uphill, leave it on the left, at a signpost (GR797 054). A stile leads into a field where you continue following the boundary to your left.

A short distance ahead a waymarker directs you left to cross a stream (a footbridge is nearby, if the stream is swollen). Bear diagonally right, uphill, making for a waymarked stile set among a small conifer plantation, (GR793 055).

Look back to enjoy the wonderful views of the Esk valley. Once over the stile head up a steep incline between the conifers to reach a second stile. Hop over this and proceed along the edge of a field, with the boundary

to your left. Again, primroses abound in spring. A television mast is evident on the left and the next objective Limber Hill Farm appears ahead (GR787 056).

The right of way skirts the left side of the farm buildings, although the farmer apparently prefers walkers to pass through the gate situated between the farm buildings. Emerging onto a road, swing left and follow its course steeply downhill, ignoring the footpath sign on the left. As you descend the red rooftops of Glaisdale village should be in view.

Towards the bottom of the hill do not turn right at a junction but continue along the road close to the River Esk. The Esk is crossed a short distance downstream by either of the bridges. There's an abundance of bridges: a road bridge, railway bridge, footbridge and the delightful packhorse bridge known locally as Beggar's Bridge (GR785 054).

This fine bridge was constructed in 1619 by Thomas Ferries, son of a moorland farmer who had become romantically involved with Agnes, daughter of a wealthy landowner from nearby Glaisdale. Agnes' father didn't approve of their liaison. This decision inspired Ferries to go to sea and seek his fortune. Eventually he returned a rich man. The lovers were subsequently reunited and married. Ferries built Beggar's Bridge as a memorial to his wife following her death many years after.

After crossing the Esk, pass under the railway then use the white painted footbridge to cross the tributary stream. Climb the steps, turning left alongside the river, walking through East Arncliff Wood which is densely

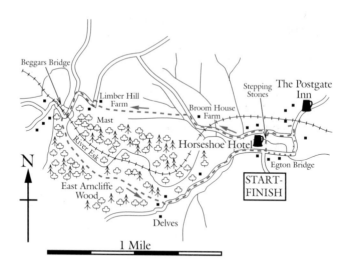

carpeted with bluebells in spring. The route follows stone trods for most of the way, part of an ancient pannier way used since monastic times.

At the top of an incline alongside this ancient highway is a memorial seat, then when the paved trod abruptly finishes continue in the same direction along a well-defined path with the Esk far below on the left. Emerging onto a road (GR793 046) at a point known as Delves, turn left and follow the road, eventually accompanying Butter Beck. Egton Bridge is entered after about 800m. Notice the datestone of 1876 inscribed on the first building. Just beyond this, turn left to the Horseshoe Hotel.

Continue along the hotel driveway to turn left down the steps before reaching the road. They lead to a double set of stepping stones across the Esk. Once over these, veer right from the weir before turning left to pass between the houses to emerge onto the road. To return to the car park simply turn right and retrace your earlier footsteps.

* Cautionary note. If the Esk is in full spate, don't attempt to use the stepping stones. Instead, return to the junction at The Horseshoe driveway and turn left along the road. A road bridge will enable you to cross the river safely. Beyond the bridge look for the Toll house which was used until the 1940s.

The Roman Catholic church at Egton Bridge is associated with the martyr Father Nicholas Postgate – the priest of the moors. Postgate was hanged, drawn and quartered at York in 1679 aged 83. His crime was being a Catholic priest on English soil when a statute of 1585 forbade this. He was born in the village and secretly administered Mass to locals between 1660-78.

Postgate would signal to the faithful by hanging out white sheets. The services were held in a building known as the Old Mass House which dated from around 1650.

In 1830 a girl accidentally broke through plaster in the building and revealed a small loft where an altar, crucifix, two candlesticks, a missal and vestments had been carefully laid out ready for Mass 150 years earlier. A visit to St Hedda's Church is strongly recommended.

BOARD INN

L E A L H O L M

ealholm, one of Eskdale's pretty villages, is an ideal spot from which to start on this wondrous journey packed with interest and superb scenery.

DISTANCE: 3¹/₂ miles
ALLOW: 2 hours
MAP: O.S. Outdoor Leisure Map 27. North York Moors, Eastern Area North East sheet
PARKING: Large car park in centre of village.

Lealholm is in the heart of the North York Moors National Park, on a pronounced bend of the River Esk. The village's charm was established at the turn of the century by Sir Francis Ley. The Board Inn is well worth a visit (TEL 01947 897279) and meals are always available.

The Methodist chapel is the oldest place of worship, celebrating its 150th anniversary in 1989. Approaching the chapel by the stepping stones, the marks on the outer wall record the levels to which the river rose on two separate occasions in past years, most seriously in July 1930. Figures on the gable ends are the work of Eskdale's local poet John Castillo (died 1845) who lived and worked in Lealholm as a stonemason. He was also a lay preacher. Close to the chapel is a long disused Quaker burial ground.

The car park opposite the church in Lealholm – often pronounced Lelhum – is the starting point for this exquisite outing. Leave the car park at its lower end and

immediately swing left before reaching the bridge to walk
eastwards along the north bank of the Esk. A signpost to
Glaisdale confirms the way. Pass alongside the cottages,
then over the cattle grid. A clear track creeps along the
valley, never far from the river Esk.

The track leads to Underpark Farm (GR772 070), where
you swing right. An Esk Valley Walk sign bearing the
salmon motif confirms the route, which threads its way
around the right hand perimeter of the farm.

Leaving the farm behind, a superb half-mile riverside
section unfurls, presenting an abundance of wildflowers
which decorate the banks in season. A stile leads into a
wooded area and to a footbridge. At a railway bridge
continue following the Esk Valley Walk signpost
downhill, still alongside the same bank of the river.

Don't cross the bridge spanning the river at GR776 067, instead clamber up the riverbank on the left towards a ladder stile where there are lots of celandines and wood sorrel at the right time of the year. Pass under the railway bridge to swing immediately left. Now follow an incline staying close to the boundary on the left. Hop over a stile close to the railway lines then make to the left side of a solitary tree in the middle of the field.

Careful observation is called for during the next section of the walk. Make towards the farmyard of Park House Farm then swing right immediately beyond a large mound of earth and to a concealed stile. From the stile head left, passing through a huge collection of redundant farming implements. At the top right hand corner of the driveway 200m away, a waymarker indicates a left turn to a second stile, hidden behind a caravan.

Cross another stile, then walk across a small enclosure towards Hill House Farm. Just short of the farm, cross another stile then veer left, along the driveway to reach the road (GR775 073) where you turn right. A short spell of road walking leads to signposts first on the right, then left which should both be ignored. As the road begins to climb leave it at a signpost and stile on the right.

From the stile proceed straight ahead across a field to reach a boundary fence. After accompanying the boundary some way, the right of way takes a direct line across the next field. Head north-east (to the right) away from the farm buildings of Lealholm Hall Farm, where waymarking is non-existent, gates are securely fastened and stiles fortified with barbed wire. Reaching the farm track, turn left, then when the track veers left towards the

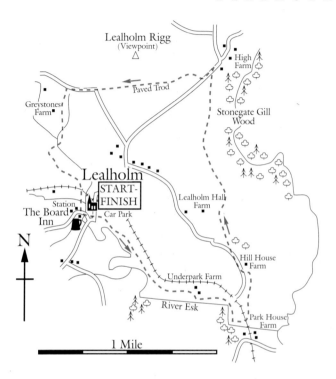

buildings, turn off right to follow the wall on your right, walking carefully along the edge of a field. The farm should now be standing across a large field to your left.

The next obstacle is a rather difficult gate standing alongside a stile, which has been "fortified" with barbed wire. Cross the next field to another gateway, then continue to an open gateway. From this head diagonally right to a stile situated alongside a gate (GR774 085). Head across the area of rough, open pasture in the direction of the red roofed buildings of High Farm.

L E A L H O L M

On arriving at the main road swing left and proceed for about 250m. At this point leave the road on the right where a signpost indicates the way. After only 50m go left across the open moor of Lealholm Rigg treading an ancient packhorse trail.

This section is a delight and offers wonderful panoramic views, particularly where the tall, stone obelisk stands (GR763 087). Beyond the obelisk, continue in the same general line, but now treading a surfaced road. Ignore the rough track to your right as you leave the moor. After 300m leave the road on the left, opposite a signpost indicating a right turn across the moor and proceed downhill, walking along a rough track. The track is forsaken on the left (GR761 086) at a waymark and the way continues downhill along a pleasant, green track with Lealholm clearly in view far below.

When the track merges with another, swing right, continuing to descend. Soon the track climbs and arrives at a junction of tracks. Take the left hand fork and at the top of the short incline go left again. The way continues along a level, green sward to arrive at Lealholm railway station. The final section involves crossing the line via a white painted gate to emerge on the road in Lealholm. Turn left to the Board Inn and the car park.

HAWNBY HOTEL

HAWNBY

A lovely walk for admiring the daffodils, primroses and violets as well as an abundance of wildflowers.

DISTANCE:
5¹/₂ miles
ALLOW: 3 hours
MAP: OS Outdoor Leisure Map 26 – North York Moors, Western Area SW Sheet
PARKING: Alongside the hotel by prior arrangement, or at Hawnby Church ¹/₂ mile from village.

Hawnby is a slightly elevated village overlooked by Hawnby Hill and Coomb Hill. The inn is at the top of the hill well above the superbly-constructed Hawnby Bridge which crosses the River Rye. The inn has deservedly acquired an enviable reputation for fine cuisine and accommodation (TEL 01439 798202 – closed Tuesday lunch).

This outing could be commenced from either the hotel or close to All Saints' Church, resting just a short distance from the village. From the hotel car park turn right along the road to a junction where you should swing right and follow the road downhill, soon passing Tancred House on the left. The Tancred family figure prominently in All Saints' Church. They owned the Arden estate until it was sold to the 6th Earl of Mexborough in 1897.

Reaching the bottom of the hill, ignore the right turn and continue along the road to cross the River Rye at the delightful Hawnby Bridge. Immediately after passing Rye

Boarding Kennels and Cattery swing right, leaving the road to pass through a stile near a substantial handrail. At the time I walked this route, the footpath had been recently diverted and a notice requested walkers to follow the waymarks. The diversion leads you around the perimeter of the field, with the boundary to your right. Note the ornamental pond attached to the kennels. An intriguing selection of ducks and geese were resident when I passed by. Reaching the corner of the field swing left (still walking with the boundary to your right) and head towards two rickety barns. Beyond these hop over a stile into a lane, turning right to cross a cattle grid.

Next comes a little hard work. A steep hill richly decorated by primroses and violets in spring, rises towards Sunnybank Farm. Just as the farm comes into view, veer off the driveway on the right, passing through a gate alongside a signpost and on to a bridleway.

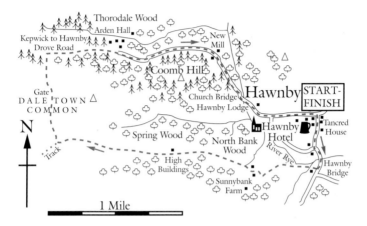

Cross the field to another gate, then turn left and right close to a well-used barn. Ignore the right turn to Dalicar Bridge and follow the sign to Dale Town Common, which is approximately two miles to the west.

Continue along the farm track which initially skirts the top end of North Bank Wood. Shortly the track veers away from the woodland and passes over Cross Dyke (GR528 894), an ancient earthwork, prior to arriving at the accurately-named barns – High Buildings. Pass either side of the barns to emerge onto a field path, which is followed through a succession of fields for about a mile to arrive at the previously mentioned Dale Town Common. A gate where the cultivated land adjoins the Common is the key to the second half of the walk. At this point swing right along a delightful springy turf pathway (GR513 894) with Bilsdale Mast, a television booster station, prominent directly ahead.

The grassy pathway eventually curves to the left and

descends to a gate. Pass through this and continue in the same direction as before, following a clear track which eventually descends towards Thorodale Woods and the Hawnby-Kepwick drove road. Turn right. The way eventually passes through woods towards Arden Hall, a 17th-century building on the site of a former nunnery which was 500 years older. Close to the hall is a metalled surface which can be followed back to Hawnby, merging at Church Bridge.

A short deviation to visit All Saints' Church is recommended. This is reached by following the track on the right, a short way after crossing the bridge. It's believed that the earliest church originated in the 12th century although the present building was extensively renovated in 1871.

During those early years the Manor of Hawnby was bestowed upon the Malbis of Acaster. Among many interesting features, the church proudly displays Hawnby's Roll of Honour, a pictorial guide taken from a copy of The Yorkshire Herald and framed. It is dated Monday October 23rd 1916 and described as being 'a proud record of a moorland parish'. There are many references to the Tancred family in the church which is best visited at daffodil time when a carpet of yellow heads swaying in the breeze, produces an unforgettable sight.

Leave the church by the main gate and turn left to the junction where a right turn will lead into the village and well-earned sustenance at the Hawnby Hotel.

THE SUN INN

B I L S D A L E

Reminders of a bygone age plus some tremendous views combine for a memorable walk above Bilsdale.

DISTANCE: 3¹/₂ miles
ALLOW: 2 hours
MAP: OS Outdoor Leisure Map 26, North York Moors Western Area SW Sheet
PARKING: At the pub.

Alongside the B1257 Helmsley-Stokesley road is a unique public house – The Sun inn, often called the Spout House. No food is served at this friendly house but the proprietors, whose descendants have owned the pub since 1823, have no objections to people eating their own sandwiches on the premises.

The Sun Inn is a homely place and spotlessly clean with the atmosphere of a public house of the 1950s. No gambling machines, juke box or piped music. An oasis of non-commercialisation! The pub originally stood at the adjacent thatched, cruck building, before the licence was transferred to the present site in 1914.

From the pub turn left and walk along the main road for approximately 400m. Reaching the entrance to Helm House Farm (and a bridleway sign) swing right to follow the driveway downhill to cross the River Seph. Beyond the river the drive rises towards the farm buildings but prior to reaching the farm turn left into a grassy lane, which passes in front of the farmhouse (GR 568 935).

The way continues along the lane, passing through a succession of gates. The easy way is to count the gates as you encounter them. After passing through the fourth gate the track leaves the wall and crosses the field heading towards gate five, which is situated alongside an oak tree. From that point the path accompanies a gritstone wall on the left, before rising up Benhill Bank (GR564 924) to pass through a conifer plantation.

Emerging from the wood, pass through a gate and then keep left at a junction of paths. Walking between stone walls a metalled surface is quickly encountered where you turn right. Follow the metalled road to Wethercote Farm (GR561 928) but go left through a gate, just short of the farm, then immediately right where there is a signpost. Head along the field towards a stile, and as you cross the field look back for a

fine, retrospective view with Easterside Hill and its little
brother Pepper Hill. From the stile continue to a gate
200m ahead, then swing left to pass through a second
gate after which select the right fork when the path splits.

*As you walk across the fields the mounds away to the left
are reminders of the former mineral workings associated
with the area. These included ironstone and whinstone,
although the principal mineral sought was jet. Others were
simply stone quarries.*

The next mile follows a delightful straight course high
above Bilsdale, passing through several gates along the
way. When you arrive at a point where the forest abruptly
ends, keep on following the same line and crossing over
an adjoining track to arrive at a gate set into a wall
(GR565 940).

*This is another wonderful viewpoint with Wetherhouse Moors
and Bilsdale Moors dissected in the valley by the River Seph
and the hamlet of Fangdale Beck nestling close by.*

From the gate commence a half mile descent, tramping
along an uneven, sunken highway formerly used for
driving livestock onto the moors for summer grazing. Far
below the square-shaped tower of Fangdale Beck church
will be seen with the pointed spire of St. John the
Evangelist church at Bilsdale Midcable.

*The latter church was founded in 1896, and was designed
by Temple Moore. An outstanding architectural feature is
the "barrel" ceiling. The tower, topped by a fine broach
spire holds just one bell. The church's clock has retained its
original movement and still has to be wound by hand.*

Reaching the bottom of the incline (GR569 945) a

cottage named
Malkin Bower is
encountered. At
this point swing
right, passing
through a
waymarked gate
to enter an
enclosed lane. The
lane leads back to
Helm House Farm,
visited earlier in
the day.

At GR573 936 pass
through a
waymarked
gate then swing
right, uphill, to
the field angle,
then veer left.

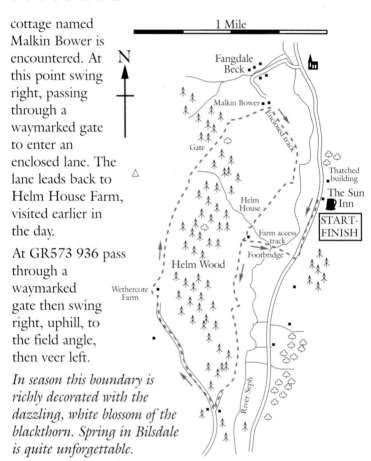

*In season this boundary is
richly decorated with the
dazzling, white blossom of the
blackthorn. Spring in Bilsdale
is quite unforgettable.*

At Helm House turn left
along the driveway to retrace
your footsteps to the Sun Inn, where the proprietor's
special brand of hospitality can be enjoyed and savoured.

BUCK INN

CHOP GATE

Superb views and hedgerows full of wildflowers make this a walk for sunny summer days.

DISTANCE:
2¼ miles
ALLOW: 1¼
hours
MAP: OS
Outdoor Leisure
Map 26. North
York Moors –
Western Area,
both SW and
NW sheets
PARKING: At
The Buck Inn,
by arrangement
(Tel 01642
778334) or the
village hall.

Chop Gate is a quiet backwater alongside the B1257 Helmsley-Stokesley road in Bilsdale. A prominent landmark is the 1,200ft television mast on Bilsdale West Moor. Chop Gate, pronounced Chop Yat, and its neighbouring village of Seave Green are overlooked on the east by a 2½ mile long earthwork.

From the Buck Inn, set out along the main road, turning right to head towards the village hall a short distance away. Cross the road bridge, noticing the village's name has been obliterated. Only the word bridge and the date 1931 remain. Perhaps this action was taken in the last war, as the threat of invasion loomed. Perhaps Chop Gate had an over-zealous Home Guard Captain?

The bridge's modern identification plate bearing Y.N.R. (Yorkshire North Riding) 782 is intact. Also close by is an ancient stone signpost with an illegible inscription. A short way beyond the bridge cross the road and hop over the stile close to the road to Esp House (GR560 994).

From the stile make diagonally right to another stile resting at the far right of the field. From there turn left and follow the road to William Beck Farm (GR569 995). The woodland away to the left is Hagg Wood.

Pass to the right of the farmhouse, then follow the waymark indicating Stonehouse Cote. The scenery is superb all around, so don't rush. On arriving at Stonehouse, pass between the farmhouse and the ancient outbuildings emerging onto the farm access track which gradually descends. Hasty Bank is directly ahead and Round Hill is on the right.

The hedgerows abound with a rich variety of wildflowers in season, as the path descends to reach the peaceful hamlet of Seave Green (GR563 003). Cross the ford or bridge and turn left to arrive at the main road.

Go straight over and enter a lane by a signpost. The path rises steeply and leads to a gate sited to the right of an old barn. Pass through the

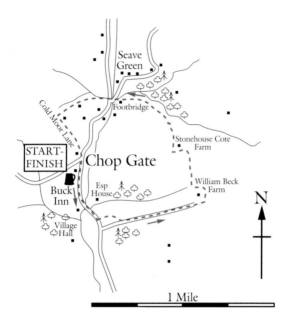

gate, then proceed straight ahead across the field to an open gateway where you swing left to enter an enclosed green lane (GR558 002).

The lane is followed back to Chop Gate and on arriving there one of the first buildings encountered is the Wesleyan chapel, erected in 1858. Notice also the granite setts underfoot. Swing left beyond the chapel to emerge onto the main road where a right turn will lead back to the Buck Inn. The village war memorial is across the road, and lower down there is a building which was obviously the blacksmith's forge.

HAMBLETON INN

HAMBLETON

Perhaps lacking distance for the more energetic, this walk accurately compensates in other ways with the best views in the book, historical connections and good food at the pub.

DISTANCE: 3¼ miles
ALLOW: 1½ hours
MAP: OS Outdoor Leisure Map 26. North York Moors Western Area. SW Sheet
PARKING: At the pub (TEL 01845 597202) by arrangement or the National Park Centre car park at Sutton Bank.

The Hambleton Inn is the only surviving hostelry along the redundant Hambleton drove road which formerly linked Cleveland with the Vale of York. Clinging closely to the edge of the Hambleton Hills this route was followed by drovers and other travellers to avoid paying tolls on the new turnpike road.

Turn right from the Hambleton Inn and walk on the busy A170 road. After a short distance cross over, taking extreme care, to a sign for The Yorkshire Gliding Club. Follow the well-trodden route of the Cleveland Way, which leads into a wood. To your right is Easten Dike ancient drainage system.

Where the path forks, select the right hand route to follow the same line as before. Soon you'll merge with a main footpath where you should turn right. It's signposted Cleveland Way – Sutton Bank (GR516 826).

Scintillating, long distance views are presented throughout the next mile. The vale of York is spread out before

you and away in the west the flat topped hills of far off Wensleydale appear, with Penhill and Addleborough prominent. Continuing along the gravelled path veer right again when the path splits. The left hand fork goes to a telescope.

Following the right hand fork you'll soon arrive at the main road again, this time opposite the Sutton Bank National Park Centre car park. Cross over veering left towards the chevron road marker. Make towards the Cleveland Way-Sneck Yate 3 miles signpost (GR514 829). The path is well defined and it's impossible to overstate the wonderful panoramic views. On the right day this location will be hard to beat, as a terrestrial paradise unfurls, but beware of low flying gliders.

Below is Gormire Lake which legend says is bottomless. In

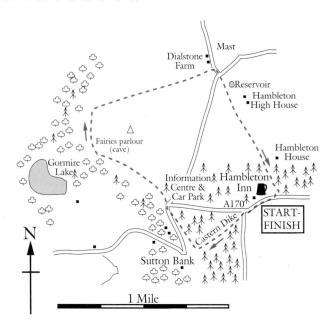

*fact the lake is filled by underwater springs and there's an
outlet at the eastern end of the lake, although the water
strangely vanishes. The adjoining Garbutt Woods are a
Yorkshire Wildlife Trust nature reserve.*

The path continues above Garbutt Wood and Whitestone
Cliff which lends its name to the village of Sutton-under-
Whitestonecliffe far below. It also passes the Fairies'
Parlour, a deep cave (GR508 837).

Ignore a turning off to the left for Gormire Lake and
keep following the Cleveland Way. Take notice of
surroundings on your right, for at the end of a small
plantation a stile leads you away from the cliff top path

and into the fields. Follow the field boundary to your right and notice the signpost to your next objective, Dialstone House. The way continues alongside a horse-racing track.

On reaching the corner of the field, turn right then left and on to Dialstone House Farm, a pristine looking establishment (GR518 843). From the farm continue on the road to a junction where you cross directly ahead. There's a footpath sign alongside the wall.

The route back to the Hambleton Inn needs little description, simply proceed in the same line. On the way you'll pass the entrances of Hambleton High House and Hambleton House farms. You'll also see a small reservoir which was surrounded with bright, yellow cowslips when I passed this way.

THE DENISON ARMS

Starting from the busy village of East Ayton near Scarborough this walk visits another of North Yorkshire's deservedly popular haunts, the Forge Valley.

DISTANCE: 4¹/₂ miles
ALLOW: 2 hours
MAP: OS Outdoor Leisure Map 27 North York Moors Eastern Area SE Sheet
PARKING: Available at The Denison Arms or nearby village hall car park.

The villages of East and West Ayton are four miles west of Scarborough on the banks of the River Derwent, at the entrance to the Vale of Pickering. The ruined castle commands a spectacular view over Forge Valley. It was a fortified dwelling rather than a true castle, dating originally from the reign of King John. The church is Norman dating from the 12th century and was founded as a chantry chapel of St John the Baptist. The doorway arch and font are of considerable historical interest.

A bridge spanning the river Derwent existed in 1492 and the present four-arched stone bridge dates to 1752. This proved inadequate to carry westbound traffic so a new-level bridge was constructed beside the old one in 1961.

Starting from the village hall car park walk along Wilson's Lane towards the junction with the main road to cross over and turn right. Notice the amusing 'Ducks crossing' sign and the old chapel bearing a datestone of

1842. Walk along the main road for a short distance to the Denison Arms. If starting at this point, leave the car park turning left. A roadside signpost indicating Cayton and Filey confirms the way. Continue alongside the busy road, passing the quaint Rose Cottage, situated just before the Parish Church of St. John the Baptist. Leaving the main road follow the boundary wall of the graveyard to Moor Road where East Ayton County Primary School is on the left.

Continue on Moor Road first passing the junction with Castle Lane then the entrance to East Ayton Lodge Hotel. At a sign indicating the road narrows turn left into a secondary lane (GR993 857). Proceed along this lane to a metal gate but don't pass through the gate, instead go into the uneven grassy track to the left.

The track heads due north and becomes somewhat overgrown, but the journey is a pleasant affair nonetheless. In summer fields of corn and barley, sprinkled with bright red poppies, adjoin on either side for much of the 1,000m section, after which you arrive at a pronounced junction (GR994 871).

At this point (a farm access track) turn left and follow the access track towards Osborne Lodge Farm (GR 987 869). Along the way a copse on the right conceals Skell Dikes, an ancient boundary or defensive system. Pass through the farm, walking between the house and the implement barn, and through a metal gate beyond the main buildings.

Continue for 100m alongside the field boundary to your left then pass through a gate and swing right. A clear woodland track leads through Ruston Cliff Wood with Forge Valley in view far below.

This valley was created towards the end of the Ice Age when a glacier extending inland from the North Sea deflected the River Derwent's original course eastwards (now known as Sea Cut) to the south. When the ice finally melted enormous amounts of water were released, forming the Forge Valley Gorge we know today. The action of the water also rendered the Vale of Pickering vulnerable to frequent flooding. To rectify that Sea Cut was excavated in the mid 19th century to divert excess water to the sea at Scalby near Scarborough. Sea Cut lies about a mile north of Ruston Cliff Wood.

The path descends steadily prior to levelling out and emerging at Green Gate car park where you turn left

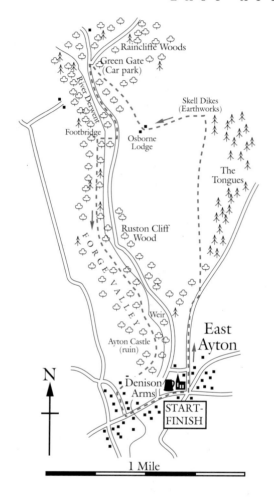

along the road (GR984 875). A notice board proclaims
the woods you've just departed are Forge Valley Woods,
although the Ordnance Survey map declares them as

Ruston Cliff Wood. This is the turning point of the outing.

After turning left again at the road junction, follow the main road beyond Bird Watchers car park, to enter Old Man's Mouth picnic site on the right. Turn right and cross the River Derwent at a footbridge, turning left along the duckboards which can be slippery when wet.

The following mile alongside the river passes through a lovely woodland alive with birdsong and embroidered with a variety of wildflowers. Bluebell time is rewarding.

As the woodland section ends, hop over the stile to leave the river, following the field/woodland boundary to your right. Alternatively, continue along the riverside until 200m beyond a weir. At that point veer right and cross the field to join the previously mentioned boundary route.

Soon the rooftops of East Ayton appear . Leave the field after rising up towards a metal gate, beyond which the track passes the ruin of a fortified tower, associated with Ayton Castle. The castle was the stronghold of the Eures family between the 12th and 15th centuries.

Conclude the walk by leaving the enclosure, walking along Castle Rise and swinging left towards the main road. Turn left again, cross the road bridge and return to the village hall car park or the Denison Arms.

BLACKSMITHS ARMS

CLOUGHTON

A superb outing enjoying the best of North Yorkshire's scenery throughout.

DISTANCE: 4¹/₂ miles
ALLOW: 2 hours
MAP: OS Outdoor Leisure Map 27 North York Moors, Eastern Area. SE sheet
PARKING: By arrangement. Tel 01723 870244.

Cloughton is on the edge of the moors at the junction of the Ravenscar and Scarborough to Whitby roads. High above the village is the old sandstone quarry which produced stone for Scarborough Castle and the small Victorian church of St. Mary. The church has a lychgate dedicated to Sir Frank Lockwood, who lived at Cober Hill, a big red brick mansion diagonally opposite the post office. He was a Solicitor General and a contributor to Punch.

Cloughton railway station, which closed in the 1960s, won many prizes for being the best kept station. Even now the roses are abundant and the hedgerows along the trackside to Ravenscar are generously decorated with colourful berries and wild flowers.

Leave the Blacksmiths Arms car park (GR008 943) and swing right along the High Street, keeping to this side of the road. Notice the old buildings which housed St. Mary's Sunday School and the Reading Room 1894, on the opposite side of the road. Another interesting feature is the wrought iron Silver Jubilee seat, located close to the pelican crossing. The village's other public house, the Red Lion, stands further up the High Street.

As the main road swings sharply left, continue in the same direction for a few paces, then turn right into Newlands Lane (GR009 947). The lane leads down to the ivy-clad Court Green Farm. Proceed in the same direction through a gateway and walk along Newlands Lane, now enjoying the agricultural surroundings. The road crosses a disused railway and soon afterwards you get the first views of the sea. Follow the road until the metalled surface abruptly ends. Close by is a seat where you can spend five minutes admiring views across Cloughton Wyke.

The walk continues northwards following the undulating coastal path known as the Cleveland Way. After a set of steep steps wonderful retrospective

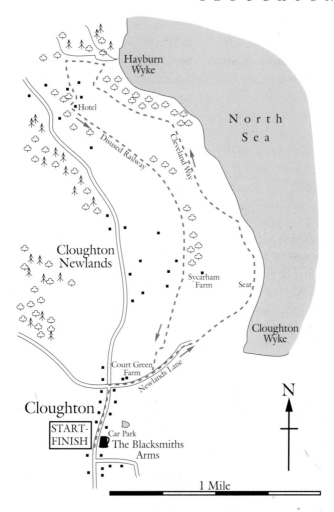

views of Scarborough Castle and several intervening bays or wykes can be enjoyed. The coastal path leads on, offering splendid views of Hayburn Wyke (GR011 971).

A visit to the beach is worthwhile and achieved by turning right at a set of waymarks and down the steps.

After visiting the stony beach onto which Hayburn Beck empties by twin waterfalls, retrace your footsteps as far as the Cleveland Way sign on the left, but continue straight ahead ignoring the Cleveland Way route. Soon the main track veers left but again follow your original line and climb steadily uphill. A faint daub of yellow paint on a nearby tree and well-worn steps, confirms the route.

Hayburn Beck tumbles down over gritstone rocks in a fine cascade where fossils of liverworts, ferns and cycads can be found. The large pebbles originally eroded from the cliffs have been jostled around by the tides, providing an excellent example of a "pocket" beach. In Victorian days special excursions from York and Scarborough brought people to visit Hayburn Wyke woodlands and to have their teas at the nearby hotel. Up until the early sixties visitors arrived by train at Hayburn Wyke station, which was situated along the now defunct Scarborough to Whitby line.

From a notice board cross a stile alongside a large gate to enter a field, then turn left and head towards a second gate beyond which lies the Hayburn Wyke Hotel. Pass in front of the hotel and continue along the main driveway ignoring the grassed track to the left. After 250m turn left through a gate onto the former railway track.

Follow the track for an enchanting 1^1/$_2$ miles to a bridge where you should leave the track on the right to emerge on the road used on the outward leg of the walk. To return to the Blacksmiths Arms simply retrace your footsteps via Newlands Lane and High Street.

ROYAL OAK

This is the walk for the high-level fraternity. Roseberry Topping and Captain Cook's Monument are included. Save this one for a fine day.

DISTANCE: 7 miles
ALLOW: 3¼ hours
MAP: OS Outdoor Leisure Map 26 North York Moors Western Area NW Sheet
PARKING: Opposite pub, alongside information centre.
Meals available at the pub, tel 01642 722361 for opening times.

Evidence of habitation in Great Ayton dates from Anglo-Saxon times. This was confirmed by the discovery more than a century ago of Anglo-Saxon crosses dating from the 8th century in the vicarage garden. The parish church All Saints was built in 1876 to replace a Norman construction where Captain Cook's mother and five of her children are buried. That graveyard forms part of the Captain Cook Heritage Trail, visited by thousands each year.

Throughout the 18th century Quakers were prominent in Great Ayton's development. They established a Meeting House in 1700. In 1841 Thomas Richardson endowed Ayton British School (now the library) and he also founded the Friends' School, which was originally an agricultural school for Quaker children.

In 1972 when local government boundaries were being re-drawn, the inhabitants of Great Ayton furiously challenged their village being transferred from Yorkshire into Cleveland. Their united efforts were successful and a village gala was

arranged by way of celebration in 1973. The gala has
continued on alternative years ever since.

From the car park almost opposite the Royal Oak turn
right along Newton Road. After 100m, soon after
passing Rosehill Theatre, turn right and cross the road to
a footpath sign. The way continues across several fields in
a straight line, following a well-defined footpath to arrive
at the Middlesbrough–Whitby railway line (GR571 112).
Along the way are the first views of Captain Cook's
monument. Cross the railway and follow the same line as
before across a tarmaced road and a stile directly beyond.
From the stile keep close to the boundary and head up
the field towards Cliff Ridge Wood. Throughout this

section are superb views of the Cleveland Hills.

Reaching an angle of the boundary (GR574 114) swing left and hop over the stile to enter Cliff Ridge Wood. After a few paces cross the main track, following a narrow track rising diagonally to the right. Cliff Ridge Wood was the site of a substantial whinstone quarry.

At the top of the incline a stile leads into a field where you turn left. Roseberry Topping, the initial objective, should be prominent at this point. After 20m, at a group of larch trees, turn right, walking directly towards Roseberry Topping.

Cross over a stile, continuing in the same direction, then soon after passing a house on the right locate a stile situated alongside a gate. At this point swing right, crossing the stile to walk along the edge of a field, with the hedge to your right. Straight ahead the presence of a gazebo promises fine views. After walking in a straight line along the edge of two fields adjacent to Newton Wood, a stile gives access onto an open hillside (GR578 125). A short but steep climb follows.

When the terrain levels out the gazebo, known as the Shooting Box, is obvious across to the left. It was erected in the late 18th century by Commodore Wilson, of Ayton Hall, and restored in 1983. Just beyond this point Roseberry Topping seems to take on Matterhorn proportions.

A small wooden gate gives access to the summit. The climb may be exhausting but the outlook will adequately compensate. The sprawling mass of Middlesbrough lays before you with Guisborough and Saltburn-by-the-Sea

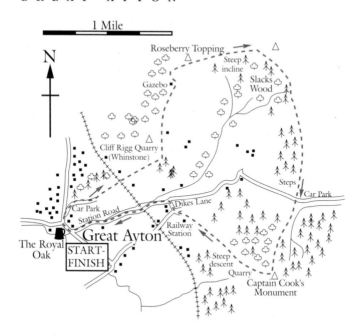

included in wonderful panoramic views. Allow about 1-
1¼ hours to this point.

Leave the summit heading eastwards along the 'cobbled'
Cleveland Way track, which soon descends quite steeply.
After approximately ten minutes a fine inscribed stone –
Cleveland Way 1995 will be seen. Continue following the
same line along a pleasant green track between a stone
wall to your right and a wire fence on the left. As the
cobbling resumes the path climbs once more towards
Slacks Wood conifer plantation.

At the top of the incline (GR588 127) follow the pointer
to Gribdale. The route follows the wall to your right,

with the vast expanse of Great Ayton Moor unfolding away on the left. In due course you descend and meet a forestry road where you go right, then after 20 paces, left, to enter Cleveland Forest (GR592 110).

The forest track leads unerringly up to Captain Cook's monument (GR590 102) erected in 1827 by Richard Campion of Whitby. It stands 51ft (15m) high at an exposed location which offers wonderful panoramic views. Allow 2-2^1/$_2$ hours to this point.

The route back to Great Ayton commences from the monument and care must be taken in selecting the correct path as there are several. A foolproof method is to stand with your back to the inscription side of the monument then walk straight ahead, following a narrow, grassy track for just a few yards. Swing right at the first opportunity to follow the less prominent of two tracks, soon passing above a redundant quarry.

Beyond the quarry pass between two upright stone posts and turning left by a waymark enter Ayton Banks Wood. A steep descent follows, keeping to the main path all the time. The path crosses over a main thoroughfare as it nears the bottom end of the wood to emerge into a field (GR584 104).

Leave the woods to follow the wall on your right to pass through a small, waymarked gate. An enclosed lane emerges at a junction with Airey House Lane, Dikes Lane and Station Road. Turn left to follow Station Road back into Great Ayton. As you approach the village note the "pissoir", a maroon painted public toilet preserved and maintained under an ancient by-law.

QUEEN CATHERINE

A walk crammed with interest. Allow extra time if you take in Mount Grace Priory – there's much to see and enjoy.

DISTANCE: 5¹/₂ miles
ALLOW: 3 hours
MAP: OS Outdoor Leisure map 26. North York Moors Western Area SW Sheet
PARKING: Roadside.

Osmotherley is a beautiful, well-tended village less than a mile east of the busy A19 road. The village has an air of local pride and friendliness, despite having become something of a tourist attraction in recent times. Earlier settlers presumably found the location a pleasant place too. Just a mile or so to the north-west, a group of Carthusian friars founded Mount Grace Priory in 1398. An opportunity to visit the well-preserved ruins is presented during the ramble.

In 1515 Catherine of Aragon, first wife of Henry VIII, established the chapel of Our Lady of Mount Grace, a short distance north of the village, known affectionately as Lady's Chapel.

At the centre of the village the ancient market cross confirms that Osmotherley was once a market town. Alongside the cross is a stone table on which John Wesley stood and preached during one of his visits in 1754.

Osmotherley is also the official starting point for the Lyke Wake Walk, a 40-mile moorland tramp across the highest ground in the North York Moors which has to be completed in 24 hours. Nothing quite so demanding here.

A good starting point is the market cross in the centre of the village, close to the Queen Catherine Hotel (TEL 01609 883209 Food Served throughout the year – check winter availability). Head along the road in the direction of Northallerton, passing the hotel on your left.

On the right is an old cottage named The Hermitage (1757) which bears a Sun insurance plaque, reminding us of the times when insured properties had to be identified. A building on fire without such a plaque would be left to burn!

Immediately after passing the Old Police House turn right into a lane. A signpost indicates the way (GR454 972). Don't miss the wonderful example of topiary

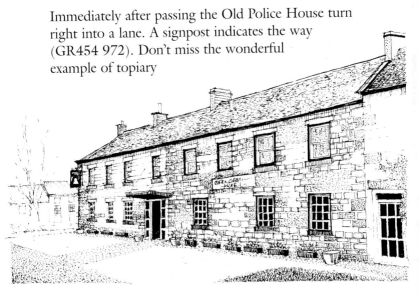

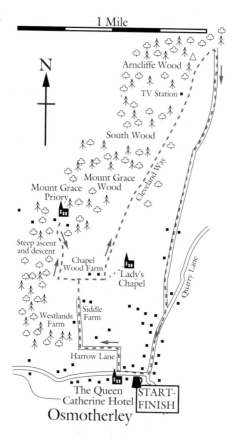

which appears soon afterwards, as the lane bends left. Soon the lane bends right and passes the entrance to Westlands Farm, continuing in a straight line beyond Siddle Farm to arrive at a waymarked gate. Pass through the gate and continue in the same direction along the field edge to arrive at a stile situated at a junction of paths (GR450 979). This is the point of the walk, a mile from Osmotherley, where options are presented.

Those wishing to visit Mount Grace Priory turn left and walk along the field edge to a stile at the bottom left hand corner (GR448 980). This gives access into Mount Grace Wood. A waymark shows the way down a clear, well-used track. An abundance of wildflowers – bluebell, wild garlic, red campion – decorates the way to a footbridge where you turn right, then negotiate the stile which leads into a car-park and Mount Grace Priory (there is an entrance fee).

The priory was founded by the Carthusian Order in 1398 and is the only Carthusian establishment in Yorkshire, housing approximately 24 monks. They lived a fairly comfortable life, each monk having his own two storey cell with food, fire and running water provided by lay brothers.

To resume the walk retrace your footsteps through the wood, over the stile and back to the original options, point. Continue straight up the field to pass through a metal gate (GR451 979) then go diagonally left across the pasture towards Chapel Wood Farm to a wooden waymarked gate. A few paces beyond the gate turn right, walking in front of the buildings to a second waymarked gate (GR453 980). Pass through the gate, continue beyond the farm buildings to another gate and head off on a wide track in the direction indicated by the Cleveland Way signpost.

A secondary track to the right leads to Lady's Chapel – another detour to consider. Whatever your decision, the walk continues from the aforementioned gate, treading the wide track that offers fine views of the surrounding countryside.

Eventually you arrive at a gate (GR455 986) which gives access into South Wood. Once inside the wood, turn right, your way confirmed by a Cleveland Way sign. A well-defined track rises steadily and presents far-reaching views to your right. In time you are confronted by an unavoidable blot on the landscape in the form of a wireless and television station situated 982ft (299m) above sea level. Beyond the station the wood's name changes to Arncliffe Wood.

Leaving the station behind follow the path for approximately half a mile to a gate (GR461 999). Pass through the gate then turn hard right (ignore a second gate) to walk along a pleasant grass track with the wall on your right. Bilsdale mast away to the left (east) will have been prominent for some time. Depending on the day, far off Roseberry Topping and Captain Cook's monument will be visible. The prominent mound in the valley to the north is Whorl Hill.

The grass track soon merges with a metalled road to the wireless station. Swing left and follow the road back to Osmotherley. Along the way Cod Beck reservoir will be observed far below on the left.

MOORLANDS HOTEL

A good outing which should stimulate appetites in more ways than food. Westerdale's church and Hunter Stea Bridge are architectural gems.

DISTANCE: 8 miles
ALLOW: 4 hours
MAP: OS Outdoor Leisure Map 26 North York Moors Western Area N.W. Sheet
PARKING: Roadside close to hotel Tel 01287 660206.

Castleton, formerly a fortified village, has retained a position of importance in the surrounding area. It formerly hosted a cheese fair each October when it's said the length of the village was lined with cheese wagons. This indicated the importance of cheese production in the region.

Hawthorn Cottage, which also functions as a bank, is where the legendary Hand of Glory originated. This was a human right hand, taken from someone who had been hanged. The hand was thought to carry magical powers which assisted burglars by ensuring victims never awakened during their sinister deeds. The hand is on display at Whitby Museum.

This is an exciting outing, full of interest and visiting three separate dales – Esk Dale, Danby Dale and the reclusive Westerdale.

From the pub turn right into the village. Pass another pub, the Downe Arms, and the Castleton Tea Rooms, then after passing Robin Hood Close take the next right turn into Ashfield

Road. This road twists and turns as it threads its way alongside Danby Low Moor, then soon after leaving Castleton the road forks – turn right.

The road which is followed is the access to Brookfield Farm (GR691 075) and passes between the house and some poultry sheds. Follow the driveway beyond the house, then as the last building is approached swing left, leaving the drive to walk across a field to a waymark close to a tiny footbridge. Cross the bridge then head off slightly right, uphill, towards a tall tree at the top of the mound. From this spot veer right making towards a signpost and a five bar gate.

Now follows a colourful mile of well waymarked meadow, through a dozen enclosures to a metalled road. Along the way Castleton Rigg will be obvious away to your right. Nestling beneath the Rigg is a sprinkling of farms. A solitary tree indicates when the final field has arrived and the route alongside the trees on your left should be followed to the gate (GR692 064).

Emerging from the field proceed straight ahead along a narrow road signposted Blakey. This leads to West Green Farm and Plum Tree Farm then terminates, continuing as a pleasant, almost straight grass track, visiting West Cliff Farm, Blackmires Farm and finally Stormy Hall (GR688 044) where you turn right – uphill.

Superb views of Danby Dale open up to your left as you climb the hill from Stormy Hall. At the summit cross straight over the main road and follow the track indicated as a public bridleway. While at this wonderful elevated position enjoy the outlook and pinpoint the two immediate objectives – Dale Head and Broad Gate farms.

Now follows a steep, moorland descent towards Dale Head (GR678 044). There are plenty of waymarks to steer you through the confines of this delightful farm. Notice the wonderful architecture of the buildings and just to the rear of the farm don't miss a real gem – the Bee House. This was constructed in 1832 as a shelter for bee skeps, the straw-built forerunners of the traditional hive. An information plaque reveals the history.

Turn right immediately beyond the Bee House. Everything's well waymarked as the path descends to cross Tower Beck by a footbridge (GR 675 045) and continues across several fields to Broad Gate Farm.

Pass the farm then continue along the farm driveway for almost 400m to a gateway where there is a tiny stile set into the wall on the left

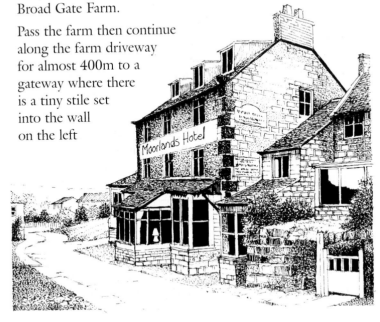

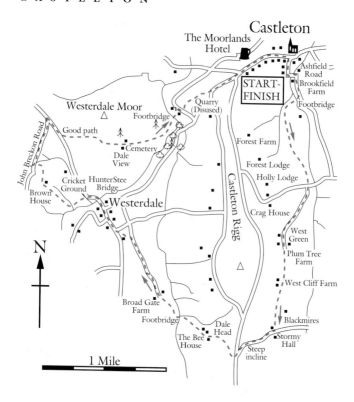

Castleton

The Moorlands
Hotel

Ashfield
Road

Brookfield
Farm

START-
FINISH

Footbridge

Quarry
(Disused)

Westerdale Moor

Footbridge

Good path

Forest Farm

Cemetery

Dale
View

Forest Lodge

Holly Lodge

Cricket   HunterStee
Ground   Bridge

Brown
House

Westerdale

Crag House

West
Green

Castleton Rigg

John Breckon Road

Plum Tree
Farm

West Cliff Farm

N

Broad Gate
Farm
Footbridge

Dale
Head

Blackmires

The Bee
House

Stormy
Hall

Steep
incline

1 Mile

(GR668 056). After crossing the stile stand with your
right shoulder facing the wall, then head off diagonally
left to a telegraph pole. Beyond this cross a seven-step,
stone stile, proceeding in the same direction to an open
gate, then a second gate leading out to the road. At this
point turn left, then right at the junction to enter the
village of Westerdale (GR664 058).

The ancient church of St. Michael and St. George is on
the left of the road facing a row of cottages. Follow this

road out of the village (ignoring the right turn signposted to Castleton) heading in the direction of Kildale.

As the road descends and a road sign indicating a ford is encountered, make a short deviation to the right to the ancient packhorse bridge known as Hunter Stee Bridge. The bridge, which spans the infant Esk, was used by packhorse trains transporting salted fish and wool to the West Riding. The bridge was restored in 1874.

Returning to the road continue downhill as before across the ford, then swing left at a footpath sign. Proceed around the left side boundary of a cricket field to a stile, then continue across a rough pasture towards a footbridge. Don't cross the bridge, instead turn right and walk uphill crossing several rough and unwaymarked pastures to Brown House Farm (GR656 065).

A colourful garden awaits summer ramblers with wild roses, honeysuckle and lilies abounding. A waymarked stile leads you into the garden, where you must keep left of the house, signposted Kildale and Stocking House. Pass through the gate alongside the house, then turn right alongside the wall.

After the short, steep uphill section use a stile just beyond a depression which leads onto the moor. Over this turn sharp left, to follow the wall soon merging with John Breckon Road. Turn right and follow this tarred road to a junction (GR656 072) where you turn right. After 400m turn left at a public footpath sign. A faint but well-used track passes across Westerdale Moor to Dale View Farm (GR666 068).

Walk along the driveway, passing between the parking
bay and the farmhouse, prior to turning right through a
gate at a signpost. Walk straight ahead for 20 paces, then
swing left to pass through another gate. Note the tiny
overgrown cemetery on the right marked with a
decorative wrought-iron gate. Two further gates are
negotiated in quick succession, then having passed
through a third follow the sign to Castleton. At the next
open gateway go diagonally left to a stile leading onto
the moors, signposted Castleton. From there simply
follow the wall which leads to a well-defined, bracken-
enclosed track which descends to a wide footbridge
(GR673 074). The day we walked this route we saw a
woodcock here.

Beyond the footbridge climb the incline and swing right
at the junction to follow a clear grassed track. Ignore the
signpost indicating a left turn. At a road turn left then
immediately right to follow another grass track around
the top of a redundant quarry, soon emerging onto
another moorland road. Turn left and follow this road
back to Castleton. Fantastic views reveal themselves along
the way.

THE LION INN

This is one of my favourite walks. The history of the ironstone industry is fascinating and this walk brings the rambler into contact with those far-off days.

DISTANCE: 7¹/₂ miles
ALLOW: 3¹/₂-4 hours
MAP: OS Outdoor Leisure North York Moors Map 26 Western Area SW Sheet
PARKING: At the premises. Tel 01751 417320.

Blakey Ridge is the high, undulating ground separating Rosedale and Farndale. The Lion Inn stands along the ridge at 1,325 feet above sea level. It's in a remote location but the hospitality doesn't suffer.

The inn is thought to have originated in the 16th century but man's presence in the region goes back much further. To the rear of the pub is Cockpit Hill or Blakey Howe, a neolithic burial mound. Other ancient edifices like Fat Betty and Ralph's Cross (the National Park emblem) illustrate evidence of continuous travel across the wild, windswept outcrops of Blakey Ridge.

From the large car park turn right along the road. After 50m turn left at a signpost for the first moorland section of the day. The scenery here is particularly colourful in mid-August when the heather is in bloom. A clear track drops down to the disused railway associated with ironstone mining. Take the right fork when the path splits close to a field boundary angle (GR682 996) then turn right at the railway, walking in a southerly direction.

Follow the railway track for 400m then, just beyond a black and white post on the left, you'll arrive at a cross-roads where a broad track crosses the railway. Turn left on the twisting track which descends to Moorlands Farm (GR692 989). Pass through a gate, then continue through the farm, turning left to reach a second gate at the rear of the main buildings.

Continue along the lane towards Hollin Bush Farm, but before reaching the house, swing sharp right and through a waymarked gate. Beyond the gate turn left and follow the wall to the far end of the field to a concealed footbridge. Cross the footbridge and turn right for ten paces, then make towards the farmhouse keeping to the left of a telegraph pole. Two gates are encountered.

On reaching the road turn left towards Dale Head Farm (GR696 993) but don't go as far as the farmhouse,

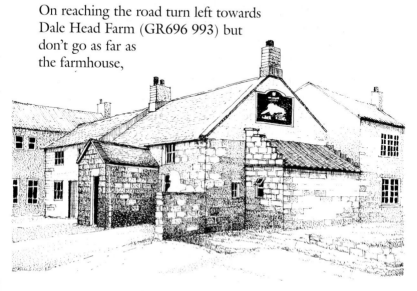

instead turn right on a bridleway signposted Great Fryup Dale. The track skirts around the right of the barn and rises steeply, to join another section of disused railway where you turn right (GR698 998). Notice the graveyard for Land Rovers as your ascent gets underway.

Now follow two miles of spectacular, high level scenery and a glimpse of Rosedale's former ironstone industry as the route takes in the East Mines site. Over a long period the more observant inhabitants of Rosedale noticed lightning frequently struck a cliff close to Hollins Farm (4 miles SE). It transpired that the outcrop was a thick band of pure ironstone, which of course was highly magnetic.

As you approach the first kilns, be aware of the incline on your left. Presumably, engines pulled ore-laden wagons along here for their contents to be 'tipped' from above into the roasting ovens or kilns. Next are the superbly-constructed 16-arch furnaces and the chimney. Thankfully, remedial work is underway in a bid to prevent further dereliction.

The railway section ends abruptly and the way continues along a gravelled path which twists and leads to a gate. Pass through this, and the farmyard soon after, and descend to a road (GR708 976). Go across the road at a signpost and walk along a lane. Pass the tidy gardens of Bracken Bank, then four private garages to enter an enclosure. A footpath sign indicates the way downhill to another gate.

From here walk across the centre of the field towards a gap in the hedge. Blakey Ridge, your return route, is high above slightly to the right. A little footbridge

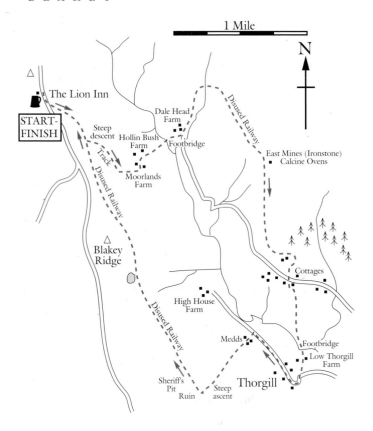

alongside a tree leads to a paved trod across the meadow. Another footbridge (GR710 968) gives access into a field used by campers. Follow the signpost through Low Thorgill Farm then continue along the driveway, turning right at the first opportunity, then right again at the road.

Follow the road through the hamlet of Thorgill, ignoring the temptation to visit Farndale when it arises, but note the Edward VII post box along the way. The metalled surface gives way to an uneven track after some distance and after passing through a wide gate the path splits. Take the left fork which passes Medd's Farm (GR704 969). Turn left behind the main building to a wooden gate alongside a barn. A stiff climb follows, initially alongside the wall to the right side.

At some obvious ironstone excavations (over the wall) a faint path parts company with the wall. Head towards the horizon and you'll find the disused railway again. Another clue is a solitary rowan tree which you should keep on your left side as you ascend the sketchy path to the railway. Turn right on reaching the railway at a point known as Sheriff's Pit. After two miles the cross-roads passed earlier are encountered and from that point simply retrace your steps to the Lion Inn. A tiny pile of stones on the left marks the exit from the railway.

The concluding railway section presents superb retrospective views of East Mines and also dramatically illustrates the areas which were mined along the western side of the valley, immediately below the railway trackbed being used for the homeward leg.

The extraction of ironstone from Rosedale started in 1856 and the previously peaceful backwater of Rosedale was suddenly transformed into a highly-productive and industrialised region, employing hundreds of men. Initially ore was transported by ponies but by the 1860s a single track standard gauge railway had to be laid, linking Rosedale Bank Top with Battersby, 14 miles to the NW. Five years later a spur was laid to East Mine. Rosedale's ironstone industry closed in 1929.